Charles Hillman Brough

Charles Hillman Brough

A BIOGRAPHY

Foy Lisenby

THE UNIVERSITY OF ARKANSAS PRESS
FAYETTEVILLE • 1996

00 99 98 97 96   5 4 3 2 1

Designed by Ellen Beeler

⊗ The paper used in this publication meets the minimum requirements of the
American National Standard for Permanence of Paper for Printed Library Materials
Z39.48-1984.

Library of Congress Cataloging-in-Publication Data

Lisenby, Foy, 1933–
    Charles Hillman Brough : a biography / Foy Lisenby.
        p.   cm.
    Includes bibliographical references and index.
    ISBN 1-55728-411-3 (alk. paper)
    1. Brough, Charles Hillman, 1876–1935. 2. Governors—Arkansas—Biography.
    3. Arkansas—Politics and government—To 1950.
    I. Title.
    F411.B85L57   1996
    976.7'052'092—dc20
    [B]   95-25687
                                                                          CIP

To Janelle and Ken

Acknowledgments

My interest in the life and work of Charles Hillman Brough covers a period of more than twenty years, and in my research and writing about him I am indebted to many people at a number of institutions and agencies. For example, I received valuable help from the history commissions of Arkansas and Mississippi, and the Latter-day Saints' archives at Salt Lake City. I am grateful also for the use of libraries of the following institutions: the University of Arkansas at Fayetteville, the University of Arkansas at Little Rock, the University of Central Arkansas, Mississippi College, the University of Utah, and Central Baptist College. In addition, I appreciate the use of materials on file at the Arkansas Baptist headquarters in Little Rock. I thank the University Research Council at UCA for financial assistance in travel and research.

Although I am unable to list everyone who assisted me in gathering materials and preparing the manuscript, I want to say a special word of thanks to the following: John Ferguson, Russell Baker, Price Roark, Sam Sizer, Ethel C. Simpson, Michael Dabrishus, Tom Dillard, Greg Urwin, Bill Larsen, Harry Readnour, Offie Lites, Willie Hardin, Carol Griffith, and Donna Johnson.

Contents

Preface

Many years ago while doing research on Arkansas topics I frequently ran across the name Charles Hillman Brough. When I investigated the state charities and corrections conference, I found that Brough supported its goals; when I looked into the status of public education, I learned that he spoke often in favor of educational reforms; when I surveyed the state's image problem, I found that Brough was an ardent defender of Arkansas's good name. Curious about the man whose name kept cropping up in my research, I began to read more about him.

Brough (pronounced "Bruff") served as governor of Arkansas from 1917 to 1921. His program was progressive, and he succeeded in getting the general assembly to enact a number of reform measures. He was also a loyal supporter of President Wilson's foreign policy, and as "war governor of Arkansas," he made hundreds of patriotic speeches, and in other ways spearheaded the "home front" in Arkansas.

Outside the realm of politics, Brough was quite an interesting figure, also. He obtained a Ph.D. from Johns Hopkins University and went on to become a popular college professor before entering politics. As a stirring orator of the "old style," he had a spellbinding effect on audiences both in Arkansas and throughout the country. He was a religious man and a prominent church leader; and, as noted above, he was a staunch defender of Arkansas against its detractors.

This biography is a brief overview of these many facets of Brough's life and work.

CHAPTER 1

Early Life and Education

*D*R. CHARLES HILLMAN BROUGH, Arkansas's progressive governor from 1917 to 1921, has been aptly described as not only a statesman but also an educator, an orator, and a Christian gentleman. He was one of the state's most fervent and dedicated boosters, devoting much time and energy to promoting Arkansas and refuting its critics.

This eloquent champion of Arkansas was actually a native of Mississippi. Most of his youth was spent in Clinton, where he was born in 1876. Growing up in this small college town, his mind and character were largely shaped by the Southern Baptist faith, the prevailing "white supremacy" racial philosophy, and the high regard which his family placed on education.

Throughout his life Brough maintained that he was a genuine southerner, "to the manner born." However, his genealogical roots were not southern. Both his parents were born in the northeast; his great-uncle John Brough was the pro-Lincoln, pro-war governor of Ohio from 1863 to 1865; the aunt and uncle who raised Brough from age six to adulthood were originally from New England, having migrated to Clinton prior to the Civil War.[1]

The father of the future Arkansas governor was Charles Milton Brough, born in Adams County, Pennsylvania, in 1842, the youngest of five children. He served in the Union army, attaining the rank of brevet captain of the Fifteenth Pennsylvania Volunteer Cavalry. During the war he was stationed for a time at Vicksburg, Mississippi. There he met Flora Thompson, his future bride, who was a teacher of English and music at the Central Female Institute at Clinton. Flora was born in Maine in 1846, but soon after her birth the family moved to Mississippi. Her sister Adelia was the wife of Dr. Walter Hillman, owner and president of the institute. Flora and Captain Brough were separated for several years, but renewed their courtship in the 1870s. Like many Americans, Brough was drawn westward in the postwar period.

The 1870 census lists him as a store clerk in Wyoming Territory, but he soon moved southward into Utah. There he was reunited with Flora, who had traveled westward to visit her brother. They returned to Clinton, where Flora was by that time principal of the institute, and were married on April 5, 1875. The couple remained in Clinton until after the birth of their son, Charles Hillman, on July 9, 1876. Within a few years they were once again in Utah, where a second son, Knight Milton, was born in 1879.[2]

Little information survives regarding the Brough family's circumstances, although the 1880 census indicates they resided in Salt Lake County and were affluent enough to afford a household servant. In 1882 Hillman (as he was referred to by family) and Knight were placed in the care of Mrs. Brough's sister Adelia and her husband, Dr. Walter Hillman, while the boys' parents remained in Utah. Reasons for this decision, like so much of the family history, are matters of speculation. The explanation usually given is that the Broughs wished to provide their sons with the excellent educational advantages of growing up in the college town under the guidance of their distinguished aunt and uncle, who would see to their proper character development as well as their academic training. Perhaps Mrs. Brough's health was also a factor; three years after placing her sons in the Hillmans' care at Clinton, she traveled to Providence, Rhode Island, in hopes of recovering from an illness, but died just three weeks following her arrival.[3]

After his wife's death, Charles M. Brough remained in Utah, evidently pursuing banking and mining interests. He lived in Salt Lake City for a while, then moved northward about thirty-five miles to Ogden, a town which had enjoyed steady economic progress as the "Junction City" located strategically near the point where the Union Pacific and Central Pacific had joined to form the first transcontinental railroad line. Within a few years Captain Brough emerged as a prominent figure in Ogden business and politics. He married Cora Stevens around 1889, and a daughter, Ruth, was born to them in 1890.[4]

Meanwhile, the Brough boys were in good hands in Clinton under the tutelage of Aunt Adelia and Uncle Walter. Dr. Hillman, a native of Massachusetts, was both an educator and a preacher. After receiving a Master of Arts degree from Brown University, he taught mathematics and natural science for two years at Mississippi College in Clinton. While at Brown he met Adelia Thompson, also a student there, and they were married in 1855. The following year Hillman accepted the presidency of the Baptist church's Central Female Institute which was located near Mississippi College. He served as president until his death in 1894. In 1891 the institute's board of trustees changed the name of the school to Hillman College, in appreciation for the long years of service of both Walter and Adelia Hillman.[5]

Adelia Thompson Hillman, the eldest of eleven children, was a native of Maine. She attended a ladies' seminary in Rhode Island before enrolling in Brown University. She received her A.M. degree from Brown and afterward taught at a young ladies' seminary in Kentucky. A "cultured and refined Christian lady" and a capable and experienced teacher, she contributed greatly to the Central Female Institute's survival during the Civil War. Thanks to the efforts of Adelia and her husband, Central, unlike many southern schools, never closed its doors during those difficult years. The Hillmans also were dedicated supporters of the nearby all-male Mississippi College, another Baptist institution. For several years following the war Dr. Hillman, who received an honorary LL.D. degree from Mississippi College in 1873, served as president of both Clinton schools, dividing his time between them and teaching religion and philosophy courses at the men's college. He and Adelia managed to get Mississippi College out of debt by the early 1870s, partly through their businesslike administration and partly through solicitation of money from northern philanthropists.[6]

The Hillmans' reputation as leaders in education extended beyond their responsibilities at Central and Mississippi College. Walter was the first president of the Mississippi Teachers Association and the author of a widely circulated pamphlet promoting public school education, and Adelia was active in the Baptist State Historical Society. Both were respected for religious and moral leadership. Dr. Hillman was an ordained Baptist minister and served for a short time as pastor of the Clinton church. He became proprietor of the Female Institute in 1869, but this did not diminish the denominational character of the school. Both Walter and Adelia were actively involved in the temperance movement, Adelia serving a stint as president of the state Woman's Christian Temperance Union (WCTU) and her husband serving on a committee to petition the state legislature to prohibit the sale of liquor.[7]

The pious atmosphere of the Hillmans' home (which was also home to the thirty-plus girls who were boarding pupils at the institute) no doubt sheltered the Brough boys somewhat from the beguiling temptations of the world. Not that there were many temptations in Clinton, which was not only free of "whiskey shops," as an advertisement for the institute proclaimed, but also was headquarters of a temperance newspaper. Parents of students at both colleges could be assured that their sons and daughters were subject to "rigid but paternal discipline." At Central, for example, the girls were forbidden to correspond with unmarried males outside their families and were not allowed to attend parties or read novels.[8]

Young Hillman Brough was greatly influenced by his aunt and uncle and by the cultivated and religious atmosphere of the community. Years later he reflected on his boyhood in Clinton, which he described as the "Athens of Mississippi":

> My boyhood days in old Mississippi were extremely pleasant, and the fine educational and moral training that I had under the direct guidance of my uncle and aunt, Dr. and Mrs. Hillman, largely contributed to what little I have been able to achieve in life.[9]

Growing up in Clinton, young Brough apparently was well behaved, a proper gentleman, eager to earn the approval of family and friends. Charles Orson Cook, in an interpretive study, suggests that separation from his father caused the boy to be anxious and doubtful about his status and to try constantly to win confirmation of his worth. Whether or not this interpretation is valid, the adult Brough spent a great deal of effort in attempting to "win friends and influence people," and on the whole was quite successful at it. We do not know how frequently Charles Milton Brough came back to Mississippi to visit his sons, or whether the boys traveled to Utah in the 1880s period. That Charles Hillman held his father in high esteem is indicated in a letter to "my dear Papa" in December 1888; the twelve-year-old had earned some money picking cotton (probably for Uncle Walter), and he sent all of it to his father, along with a letter requesting that he use it to purchase ". . . a pocket-book or some nice Christmas reminder that you may keep, and remember me."[10]

Thus, as he prepared to enter Mississippi College at age fourteen, Charles Hillman Brough was thoroughly imbued with the social and religious attitudes which were pervasive throughout the South and rather widespread in other regions as well. And while the genteel climate of the Hillman household as well as the broadening influences of higher education must have effected some modification of his views, he continued in the main to adhere to them throughout his life.[11]

Mississippi College, like its neighbor, the Central Female Institute, was committed to providing Christian education; emphasis was placed on refining the spirit as well as the intellect. Students attended daily religious exercises and were strongly encouraged to participate in weekly prayer meetings and to attend public worship at some church on Sundays. Parents of the young men were assured that their sons were ". . . as safe here as when surrounded by the influence of home." Upon enrolling, students were required to make a "matriculation pledge" to obey college rules and to declare they possessed no firearms and would not acquire any while at the college.[12]

The Bachelor of Arts degree program, in which Brough enrolled in September 1890, included courses in the following fields: grammar and composition, classical literature, modern literature, mathematics, natural science, philosophy, history, and economics. In addition students were required each week to prepare and deliver "original orations and selected declamations." The two literary societies, the Hermenian and Philomathean, held debates regularly. Further evidence of the high regard for oratory was competition for prizes given each year during commencement week. Brough, who had earlier demonstrated his interest in oratory by preparing a dissertation on dirt daubers, was among the more talented speechmakers on campus; he was an active member of both literary societies and was selected by the Philomatheans to present the group's "anniversarian" oration in April 1894. He was also one of the finalists for the "Lee gold medal" oratorical competition at commencement in May 1894. Brough maintained a high scholastic standing, being listed three out of his four years as one of the distinguished students—those with an average of 95 in both scholarship and deportment. Graduating in 1894, he shared "First Honors" with another B.A. student and was the youngest man at that time to receive a bachelor's degree at Mississippi College.[13]

More than a year elapsed before Brough resumed his academic labors. He spent most of these intervening months with his father in Ogden, Utah. During the early nineties the elder Brough served as a teller in one bank and as cashier in another and apparently was also involved in the mining business. Perhaps he had come to Ogden because of a "silver boom" in the area early in the decade. Whether or not he acquired significant wealth is unknown, but he definitely emerged as a rather successful leader in the somewhat confused city politics of the period. Only recently had the Liberal party ("Gentiles") succeeded in reducing the strength of the People's party (the Mormons). In the elections of 1892 Captain Brough was elected treasurer on the Liberal ticket; indeed, the Liberal candidates carried Ogden for every office but one. In the fall of 1893, however, the Liberals, having accomplished their principal mission of curtailing Mormon political power, decided to dissolve and allow each of their members to embrace one of the two national parties. Captain Brough was an important influence in persuading the Liberals to take this crucial step. Brough himself joined the Republican party, and the local organization nominated him for mayor in the 1893 campaign. He won a very narrow victory over his Democratic opponent, becoming Ogden's first Republican mayor, serving from January 1, 1894, to December 31, 1895.[14]

Young Hillman Brough, whose college studies included history and political economy, must have been impressed by his father's political success. However, the son did not arrive in Ogden in time to witness Mayor Brough's handling of a potentially explosive problem the city faced in the spring of

1894. About one thousand members of an "industrial army"—the Far West version of "Coxey's Army"—arrived in Ogden early in April, en route to Washington, D.C., the destination of several such protest groups seeking relief from unemployment. As chronicled in the *Ogden Standard,* the mayor's handling of the situation was statesmanlike. He was instrumental in providing food for the indigent "army" during its brief stay in Ogden and played a key role in helping the group secure railway transportation for a continuation of their eastward "march." Editorials in the *Standard* lauded the mayor's actions and criticized the territorial governor, Caleb W. West, who apparently wished to force the army of unemployed men to return to California. In the summer of 1894 Mayor Brough had to cope with another crisis when Ogden, like many cities throughout the nation, felt the repercussions of the "Pullman strike." The American Railway Union, in support of a strike against the Pullman Company near Chicago, had launched a boycott against the railways' use of Pullman cars. Mayor Brough's position was similar to that of the *Standard:* he agreed that the Pullman workers were justified in their strike, but took a firm stand against the union's use of threats, intimidation, and violence to carry out their boycott of the railroads. The mayor issued a proclamation pledging severe punishment of all persons guilty of violence.[15]

Following his tenure as mayor, Captain Brough continued to exhibit leadership in civic affairs; in 1896, for example, he was among the coordinators of an elaborate July 4 celebration. In addition, the ex-mayor continued to be actively involved in Republican party activities. A major question facing Brough and a number of other Utah Republicans was whether or not to abide by the national party's decision in June 1896 to reject "bimetallism"—that is, inflating the currency through a government policy of coinage of silver. The "free-silver" idea had received its initial momentum from a third party, the Populists, but for several years the cause gained considerable support within the old parties as well. The author of the most widely read treatises advocating bimetallism, William Hope "Coin" Harvey, resided in Ogden for several years, but moved to Chicago in 1893. Many farmers throughout the South and West were convinced that inflation was the correct remedy for their distress in the depression which had begun in 1893, and as the season of conventions and nominations approached, their spokesmen in the Democratic party plotted to capture the organization for free silver in the election of 1896. This they succeeded in doing at the party convention in July. Among Republicans, the strongest support for bimetallism was found in western mining states such as Colorado and Utah. When the "silver Republican" delegates to the party's convention at St. Louis lost to the gold standard advocates in the platform struggle, twenty-one of them, led by Sen. Henry M. Teller of Colorado and

Sen. Frank J. Cannon of Utah, walked out of the convention. Cannon, who as editor of the *Ogden Standard* had promoted free silver, was apparently a friend and political associate of Charles Milton Brough, having "cheered him on" in his political campaign in 1893. Cannon and Brough were foremost in generating support for free silver in Ogden in 1896.[16]

Both Hillman and Knight Brough lived with their father in Ogden in the summer of 1896 and were employed by the Union Pacific and Rio Grande Coal Company. Hillman, who had completed his first year of graduate studies at Johns Hopkins University (1895–96), probably spent some time collecting data for his dissertation topic on "Irrigation in Utah." Before returning to Baltimore in the fall to resume his studies, Hillman began to develop more than a passing interest in the local free-silver agitation.[17]

Young Brough not only sympathized with Cannon's—and the elder Brough's—pro-silver views, but served, along with Cannon, as one of the "silver speakers" at a large rally held on September third at the Grand Opera House. The rally was attended by friends of free silver from neighboring cities as well as from Ogden and had as its main purpose the formal declaration of support for William Jennings Bryan, the Democratic presidential nominee whose "Radical" allies had won over the party for bimetallism at the July convention. Senator Cannon delivered an eloquent speech in which he declared his support for Bryan and free silver. Reporting on the meeting the next day, the *Standard* announced the birth of a new party—the Independent Republican party of Utah. The story also discussed the presentations of several orators, including that by Hillman Brough, whose address was described as "interesting and pointed," being interrupted frequently by cheers and applause. Brough implied that the gold wing of the Republicans had secured control of the convention by purchasing the votes of "124 nigger delegates" from the southern states. Denouncing this and other examples of control by the "shylocks" in the party, Brough asserted that he had "resolved not to worship the golden calf" and urged his fellow silver Republicans to rally instead to the cause of Teller and Bryan who had ". . . written the Declaration of Independence" from "shylock slavery."[18]

Perhaps this speechmaking opportunity, and the appreciative response of the audience, planted the seeds of political ambition in the mind of Charles Hillman Brough. His politics in later years was strictly and unswervingly Democratic, despite his brief flirtation in 1896 with a maverick form of Republicanism. One constant factor in his politics, both in the nineties and years afterwards, was his high esteem for Bryan, not only as a politician but also as a great orator and a Christian gentleman.

Soon after the big silver rally, which gave birth to a pro-Bryan party, the younger Brough was on the train back to Baltimore to resume his graduate studies at Johns Hopkins. He was pursuing a doctor's degree in history, political economy, and jurisprudence. Among his professors was Herbert Baxter Adams, who had been a full-time history professor at the university since 1881. Adams had received his Ph.D. degree from Heidelberg University in 1876 and was strongly committed to the scientific approach in historical studies. Adams's history seminar was modeled after that of the German universities, and he possessed the rare ability ". . . to convert a new provincial into an aspiring and assured research student and writer of history." Besides being an excellent teacher and director of research, Adams was a principal founder of the American Historical Association and the initiator of a monograph series known as the *Johns Hopkins Studies in Historical and Political Science*. Hillman Brough undoubtedly benefited from Adams's guidance, as well as that of other Johns Hopkins professors, but in later years he made most frequent references to having Woodrow Wilson as a teacher. The Princeton scholar presented a series of lectures at Hopkins, and many university students enrolled in these series for credit. Whether Brough received credit is not known, but the impression Wilson's lectures made on him was significant.[19]

While in Utah Brough did much of the research on his doctoral dissertation, "Irrigation in Utah." The project must have been virtually completed by the end of the 1896–97 school year, for in the spring of 1897 he was awarded a fellowship in political economy, based largely on the quality of his dissertation. The fellowship included a prize of five hundred dollars. In November 1897 he addressed the Maryland Academy of Science on the topic of irrigation, obviously a continuation of the dissertation research. Professor Adams and Hopkins president Daniel C. Gilman considered the dissertation a "valuable monograph," and Adams published it as a volume in his Johns Hopkins series in historical and political science. The *Washington Post* hailed the work as probably the "most complete and exhaustive study of its kind in existence." Congratulatory letters came to Brough from a variety of people, including an official of the Utah Irrigation Association, who said the study was better than any other on the subject, and promised to refer to it as the standard authority. The monograph received favorable reviews in journals, European as well as American. President Theodore Roosevelt was said to have consulted Brough's book in connection with policies on arid lands reclamation. Despite all of the accolades, however, sales of the book were slow until the young scholar, taking his father's advice, proceeded to sell copies in the Ogden area, mostly to Mormon residents.[20]

The first part of *Irrigation in Utah*, mostly historical, indicates that

Brough was an apt student of the scientific method as promoted by Adams and others. Thoroughly researched and extensively documented, this history of early Mormon settlement in the arid west draws heavily upon such primary sources as the journals and diaries of pioneer settlers. In the second section Brough identifies potential future problems for Utah in relation to water supply and proposes possible solutions.[21]

Brough performed brilliantly on his Ph.D. examinations in 1898. He wrote his father that his professors had congratulated him "as having passed a most brilliant examination, not missing a single question." Captain Brough was unable to attend his son's graduation exercises, but he sent a telegram praising his "wonderful achievements and splendid triumph." On June 14, 1898, Charles Hillman Brough—not quite twenty-two years old—was awarded a Ph.D. degree in economics, history, and jurisprudence.[22]

CHAPTER 2

Teacher, Scholar, Orator

*A*FTER RECEIVING HIS PH.D., Brough became a college professor. In the fall of 1898 he began an academic career which totalled sixteen years and included tenure at three institutions. In addition to teaching he published scholarly essays, secured a law degree, remained active in the Baptist church, and energetically used his greatest talent—public speaking. During these years he maintained his interest in both national and state politics, and in 1915 left the classroom to run for governor of Arkansas.

In his quest for a teaching position in 1898, Brough was armed with letters of recommendation from his professors describing the young scholar as "an indefatigable worker," "a student of marked ability and great promise," who was "prompt, intelligent, and thorough." Several days before commencement at Johns Hopkins, Brough learned that he had been elected professor of political economy at his alma mater, Mississippi College. His preference, however, was for a position at the University of Utah. Apparently no offer from that institution was extended, for Brough accepted the Mississippi College appointment and, following a summer visit with his father in Ogden, traveled to Clinton and assumed his first university teaching responsibilities.[1]

Judging from the Mississippi College catalog of 1898–99 these responsibilities were demanding. Brough was listed as the only professor in two "schools"—the school of psychology, ethics, and logic, and the school of economics and history. In addition to teaching his courses in these areas, Brough acquired a Master of Arts in psychology and ethics at Mississippi College during his first year. In his second year Brough assumed the role of instructor in German, in addition to his other teaching duties.[2]

The history program as described by the 1889–99 catalog indicates that the ideal of "scientific" history had taken root at the college. The catalog defined history as "past politics," and students were advised that the courses focused upon "institutional growth, constitutional progress, and religious development of nations." Although this approach to history conformed to prevalent patterns of scholarship at Johns Hopkins and elsewhere, the extent to which Brough adhered to it is not known.[3]

A letter from Professor Adams at Hopkins suggests that the young scholar was rather demanding of his students. Adams, replying to a letter from Brough, reminded him that his Mississippi College boys were not graduate students, and that they needed the elements of historical knowledge more than a philosophy of history. However, Brough was a popular teacher and was the subject of frequent "gossipy" items in the *Mississippi College Magazine*, including speculations about his bachelor status; one item suggested that considering the rush of the Hillman College girls to his Sunday School class, he should have no fear of remaining a bachelor.[4]

Academic and social life did not deter Brough from making frequent use of his oratorical ability; during his three years at Mississippi College he delivered scores of addresses on a variety of topics. A brochure circulated by a chautauqua organization on "Dr. Charles Hillman Brough, Lecturer," listed the professor's favorite subjects: "Political Problems of the Present," "The Wit and Wisdom of Great Americans," "The Glory of the Old South and the Greatness of the New," "Woman," "The Americanization of the World," "The Sunshine and Shadows of Life," "God in History, " and "We Study but to Serve." He lectured to chautauqua audiences and to religious gatherings such as the Baptist Young People's Union Convention and the Southern Baptist Convention. Brough was also kept busy giving commencement speeches— his schedule for the spring of 1899 included addresses at Burns School at Forest, Mississippi, Raymond High School, and Blue Mountain Female Academy. He often delivered addresses for patriotic or memorial occasions. The following excerpt from a July 4 oration at Magnolia, Mississippi, is representative of his grandiloquent style:

> And on this natal anniversary of our country's history, in this moment of her matchless triumphs, on this heyday of her fondest hopes, in the fullness of her rarest beauties, I wonder not that all children of Columbia's reign salute with merry voices and crackling bonfire the glorious ship of a union strong and great, flying to her masthead a flag known on every sea and honored in every clime.[5]

Brough's interest in and attachment to the Baptist church had begun years earlier as he grew up under the watchcare of the Hillmans. He continued to be active in church affairs, serving as leader of the Baptist Young People's

Union, teaching a Sunday School class, and representing his church as a delegate to the state Baptist convention in 1902.[6]

Brough's demanding classroom duties, speechmaking, and church activities did not preclude growth through research, publication, and involvement in professional organizations. Prof. Jacob H. Hollander asked him to prepare a history of taxation in Mississippi to be included in a volume on taxation in the southern states. Brough submitted his study in 1899, and Hollander published it after making only slight changes. Meanwhile, *Irrigation in Utah* continued to receive favorable attention, and a French translation of the work was published.[7]

Some of Brough's writings appeared in the *Mississippi College Magazine;* for example, "Loyalty to Mississippi," "We Study but to Serve," and "A Plea for the Extension of the Rural Free School Term." He also published articles in the *Publications* of the Mississippi Historical Society, including the essay on taxation in Mississippi and two articles dealing with the history of Clinton. He served on the executive board of the society and held memberships in the American Historical Association and the American Economic Association.[8]

The secretary of the state society, who also served as editor of its *Publications,* was Dr. Franklin L. Riley, professor of history at the University of Mississippi. Both Riley and Brough had studied under Professor Adams at Johns Hopkins, where they completed their Ph.D. programs in the 1890s. In a letter to Adams in 1901 Riley described Brough's career as "something remarkable," but this generous praise of a colleague was offset by his knowledge that Brough planned to resign his position at Mississippi College and undertake the study of law. The college board of trustees regretfully accepted Brough's resignation and passed resolutions complimenting him on his scholarship and Christian character. In August 1901 he was licensed to practice law on the basis of examinations he took; however, wishing to broaden his knowledge in the field, he entered the University of Mississippi Law School in September.[9]

Brough entered the new phase of his education with characteristic diligence and enthusiasm. He completed the two-year Bachelor of Laws degree program in one year, graduating with distinction in the spring of 1902. During the first half of this intensive year of Law School Brough found time to contribute an article on "The Ideal Student" to the university magazine. Early in 1902 he presented his paper on "The Clinton Riot" at the annual meeting of the Mississippi Historical Society. This paper, later published in the Society's *Publications,* dealt with the 1875 race riot in the Clinton area and its relation to the overthrow of "Radical Reconstruction" in Mississippi.[10]

Although much of Brough's writing, such as his dissertation and other studies on economic history, reflects the Johns Hopkins training in thorough research and objective reporting, his treatment of the Clinton Riot was marked by obvious bias against the Radical regime in Mississippi. This bias is understandable considering his upbringing in an environment which emphasized white supremacy. Moreover, the current "orthodoxy" in Reconstruction historiography was the anti-Radical approach which typified the "Dunning School" of historians. However, Brough's denunciation of the "Carpetbag Charlatan of a mongrel governmental mixture" imposed by Republican governor Adelbert Ames, seems excessive even for the times. Throughout his essay Brough used epithets and emotionally charged words, as when he celebrated the victory of Democratic home-rule over the "mongrelism, ignorance, and depravity" of carpetbagger government. Compared with Brough's biased treatment, James Garner's *Reconstruction in Mississippi*, a Dunning School monograph, is a model of scholarly restraint and objectivity. While critical of the Republican regime, Garner, unlike Brough, avoided vituperative and emotional language and was more cautious in assigning blame for the racial troubles at Clinton and elsewhere.[11]

Despite the slanted version of the disturbances at Clinton, Franklin Riley continued to have a high regard for Brough's scholarship, and in a letter of recommendation described his work as "scientific and scholarly." Riley had been a key figure in the successful campaign to secure a state department of archives and history. The law setting up this agency provided that its first board of trustees would consist of the executive board of the historical society. The board met in March 1902 for the purpose of inaugurating the new department. The most important agenda item was selection of a director, and Dr. Brough was among the three applicants for the position. One of the other applicants withdrew, leaving the board of trustees with a choice between Brough and Dunbar Rowland, a Coffeeville, Mississippi, attorney. Brough lost to Rowland by a vote of five to four and was thus obliged to start looking for a teaching position for 1902–03. He had decided not to take up the practice of law, although his study of the subject was beneficial in thoroughly preparing him to teach history and politics.[12]

Among those who wrote letters of recommendations for Brough in the spring of 1902 were three acquaintances at the university—Professor Riley of the history department, Dean Shands of the Law School, and Chancellor Fulton. Riley predicted Brough would become one of the South's distinguished educators; Shands cited his wonderful capacity of acquiring and retaining knowledge; Fulton praised his outstanding talents as a teacher and his remarkable feat of completing the law course in half the usual time. All three commended him for his high moral character. About this time Brough also received a flattering letter from Frank J. Cannon of Utah. Cannon was pleased to learn of Brough's decision to pursue a career in higher education, and predicted for him glorious achievements in behalf of humanity.[13]

Whether Brough made many applications or received many offers from 1902–03 is not known, but the one he accepted brought him back to Clinton as chair of the Hillman College Department of Philosophy, History, and Economics. The declining health of his aunt Adelia Hillman seems to have been the main factor in Brough's return to Clinton, as he thought he could help care for her. However, she died on June 30 and his homecoming was marked with sadness.[14]

Hillman College had always been a "Christian School of Culture and Refinement," and although it was independent of denominational control, the Hillmans and subsequent proprietors and managers were dedicated to promoting the Baptist faith. Like other such schools it had rigid discipline; the girls were not to "keep company with any unmarried gentlemen (cousins included) without permission from the Lady Principal . . ." They were prohibited from receiving letters from anyone except family members, without permission from parents or guardians. Some pupils thought the rules too numerous and perhaps too rigorous, as evidenced by a poem entitled "A Plea for the Ruleless School," published in a student magazine.[15]

Dr. Brough was just as popular and just as busy as he had been in the three-year tenure at Mississippi College. He continued his involvement in church activities, his oratorical appointments, and his scholarly pursuits. His reputation as a scholar, Christian gentleman, and a good conversationalist remained undiminished, and he continued to be held in high esteem by students and colleagues. However, his desire to secure a more promising position—combined, probably, with a lingering disappointment at not gaining the archives position—led him to send out applications for teaching jobs and request letters of recommendation. Those who wrote in his favor included A. M. Longine, governor of Mississippi, Dr. John L. Johnson, president of Hillman, Rev. W. T. Lowrey, president of Mississippi College, and Henry L. Whitfield, state superintendent of public instruction. All gave Brough unqualified recommendations, with Whitfield noting particularly the assistance Brough had given him in a campaign to improve the rural school program.[16]

Three university positions were offered—professor of modern languages at Mississippi College, the chair of political economy at Furman University, and the chair of political economy at the University of Arkansas. He accepted the last one, and in July 1903 moved to the state which would be his adopted home for the rest of his life.[17]

Brough joined the Arkansas faculty at a time when the institution, according to its historians, was strengthening its position and acquiring strong support among alumni and friends. The president, Harry S. Hartzog, made numerous speeches promoting the university, and during his three-year tenure was successful in securing significant increases in legislative appropriations for the university. In addition, Hartzog secured several distinguished new professors, including Brough, who immediately began to build up good enrollments in his Department of Economics and Sociology.[18]

Until 1907 Brough was the only member of the department. In that year he was joined by Neil Carothers, who had the title of adjunct professor. Purposes of the department's courses, as outlined in the university catalog for 1905–06, were

> to give instruction in problems of current economic, social and public interest, to prepare students for the duties of citizenship and participation in the professions of laws, politics, journalism, financiering in general, for professional and business careers.

The department curriculum that year consisted of principles of economics, business law, money and banking, transportation, insurance, public finance and public works, financial history of the United States, socialism and social reform, the labor question, principles of sociology, and modern methods of charity.[19]

During his first year at Arkansas Brough wrote Professor Hollander for advice on economics books to acquire (whether for himself or for the library is not known). Hollander advised him to be certain to get the classics—Adam Smith, Ricardo, Malthus—for these constituted "the real basis of the science of economics. . . ." He expressed confidence that Brough would "carry the spirit of sound method and scientific inquiry" into "his new territory." Hollander encouraged his former student to undertake the study of taxation in Arkansas and perhaps broaden it to a general financial history of the state.[20]

Brough's positive impact in the classroom during his first term was indicated in a university *Newsletter* in December pointing to the fine "showing" of the economics and sociology department: five of nineteen arts seniors were majoring in economics, while six others were taking extensive work in the field. Brough was a popular teacher, as he had been at Mississippi College and Hillman. His classes were crowded, mainly because his lectures were interesting and frequently connected to current events. He had high expectations of his students and took an interest in their affairs. His support for extra-curricular activities included making speeches at celebrations of athletic victories.[21]

Comments in the university yearbook reveal a perception of the professor as knowledgeable, polite, and perhaps a "soft touch" for good grades. The *Cardinal* for 1903–04, reporting on a (real or imaginary?) football game between seniors and faculty members, described Brough bowing politely before making a "graceful tackle." In the next year's edition he was mentioned in a feature entitled "Never in a Thousand Years"—a list of things that would never happen. One of these was Professor Brough being impolite. One of the co-eds—who later married Brough's brother-in-law—recalled his courteous and chivalrous way of addressing the young ladies, always calling them "Miss" and using their first names. An additional reason for his popularity was the fact that he had apparently relaxed his grading standards somewhat since the Clinton years when Dr. Adams (of Johns Hopkins) had chided him for being too demanding. A limerick in the 1910 yearbook indicates that he had become rather generous in handing out "E's"—the highest mark:

Doctor Brough's a failure on P's
With this point he fully agrees;
He plants them indeed
But they all are bad seed;
For when they come up they are E's.[22]

An anecdote from one of his classes pictured Brough as a man disinclined to take a firm position on issues. A student asked him his views on Theodore Roosevelt and Eugene Debs, the Socialist, and Brough responded with flattering remarks on both men. The student then asked the professor's views on the Devil, and received this reply: "The Devil is to be admired for his tenacity."[23]

President Hartzog, himself an accomplished public speaker, encouraged Brough to make addresses to high-school audiences, and the professor obliged. He was experienced at this, having made promotional speeches on behalf of Mississippi College and in favor of a stronger rural school program in Mississippi.[24]

Brough was available as lecturer for a variety of organizations—such as the University Athletic Association, the Daughters of the Confederacy, and the Ozark Land Congress. His address to the United Daughters of the Confederacy, at a meeting celebrating the one hundredth anniversary of the birth of Robert E. Lee, was described by the *Fayetteville Daily Democrat* as "masterful and eloquent"; the *University Weekly* published the speech a few days later as a page-one story. Brough praised the Confederate hero not only for his "sterling character" and "military prowess," but also for his wisdom in recognizing the reality of the South's defeat. While some ex-Confederates were bitter and vindictive,

> Lee's voice rang clear across the troubled waters, "Peace, be still."[25]

Another hero of the Lost Cause whom Brough extolled was Rear Adm. Raphael Semmes. The occasion—the one hundredth anniversary of Semmes's birth—was sponsored by the Southern Memorial Association of Fayetteville. Brough's concluding paragraph eulogized Semmes as "a Nelson without his degeneracy, a Drake without his piracy, a Sampson without his selfishness, a Dewey without his imperialism, and a martyr without his crown." Portions of the speeches on Lee and Semmes were identical; for example, Brough's explanation of the causes of the Civil War, inspirational poetry, and illustrative story from Scottish legend, et cetera. The idolizing of the southern heroes, pleasing to the sentimental audiences, was quite consistent with Brough's own high esteem for the "Southern way of life." As noted in the first chapter, he considered himself a true southerner, "to the manner born," although his parents were northerners.[26]

Brough continued to be an active church member, serving as a deacon in the First Baptist Church, teaching a Sunday School class, and occasionally "filling the pulpit"—not only for Baptist congregations, but also Catholic, Methodist, and other churches. He had a strong interest in the university YMCA, whose membership increased significantly following its formation in 1902. In 1905 Brough published a short history of YMCA activities in a campus magazine, praising the organization for its contributions toward enhancing the university's "moral tone and Christian sentiment" through Bible classes and other religious meetings. Noting that the faculty gave hearty support to the YMCA, as well as to the more recently organized YWCA, Brough expressed hope that their work would make the University of Arkansas "a beacon light of Christian influence" to the youth of the state.[27]

Until 1907 Brough's absorption in teaching, writing, oratory, and other activities had evidently allowed little time for romance. But in 1907 he met Anne Wade Roark, of Franklin, Kentucky, who was visiting her cousin and family in Fayetteville; a fervent courtship ensued and culminated in their wedding on June 17, 1908.[28]

Anne was the only daughter of Mr. and Mrs. Wade Roark. Both parents possessed excellent family trees and could trace their lineage to revolutionary times in Virginia and North Carolina. Mr. Roark was a well-known lawyer, banker, and businessman, and his family was prominently mentioned in the "society news" of Franklin. They lived in an elegant "old Kentucky home"— two storied, multi-gabled, surrounded by a wrought-iron fence. The Roarks had two sons, one of them two years older than Anne, the other eleven years older.[29]

After graduating from Franklin Female College in 1896, Anne attended the Hollins Institute in Hollins, Virginia, where she studied English literature, Latin, German, music, and harmony. Judging from a surviving grade report, she was a good student, making good marks in all her subjects, and receiving "100" in deportment. Like other young girls from affluent families, Anne did not attend college for the purpose of training for a career, but to achieve the cultivation befitting a woman of her social station. Following her collegiate training she used her musical talents as church organist for the Baptist church in Franklin. In the early 1900s her pastor, Rev. Walter A. Whittle, in a letter to Anne's mother, expressed his high regard for the young woman's Christian character and dedication to the work of the church. Whittle said that twenty-five young people like her could win all of Franklin for God and righteousness. He described her as "a joy to her Pastor's heart, a benediction to our church and an honor to society."[30]

The Brough-Roark romance seemed to progress smoothly except for a brief period in the fall of 1907. A letter to "My dear Miss Anne" on October 11 indicates that he somehow had hurt her feelings, and she was planning to return a ring and a bracelet he had given her. He apologized profusely, begging her forgiveness, and asked her to marry him. Two days later he wrote her again, this time including a poem asserting his love for her. This letter opened with "My dear Miss Anne" and was signed "Dr. Brough." The quarrel, or misunderstanding, was cleared up, and although the formal announcement of their engagement was not made until the following spring, a letter to Anne from her future father in law in December welcomed her to the family. In January the groom-to-be wrote her expressing his love and longing for the day they would marry. He quoted the words of a song called "Just a Wearyin' for You."[31]

The engagement and approaching marriage were announced at a party at the Roark home some weeks before the June 17 wedding. The Franklin newspaper gave extensive coverage of this event, as well as the wedding itself; the Roarks were a prominent family and their home was one of the city's handsomest. The marriage occurred at 7:30 P.M. on June 17, 1908, at the Baptist church. Dr. Brough's brother, Knight, his wife, and small son were present, although the groom's father and stepmother were unable to make the trip from Los Angeles. They sent messages of congratulations and extended a hearty welcome to Hillman and Anne, for the wedding trip included a visit with the elder Brough, his wife, Cora, and daughter Ruth on the west coast. Newspaper accounts of the wedding indicate the high esteem enjoyed by the newlyweds; Anne was described as "accomplished and cultured, a fair representative of a prominent Southern family," and Hillman was called a "worthy representative of a noble Southern family . . . now living in California. . . ." Since Brough's father was a native of Pennsylvania, this last information was incorrect; however, as noted in the first chapter, Charles Hillman was thoroughly imbued with "Southernism."[32]

On their wedding trip Hillman and Anne went to Lookout Mountain near Chattanooga, visited with Knight and family in Vicksburg, then embarked on the long train trip to California. On the way Dr. Brough filled several chautauqua engagements in Oklahoma. Soon after they arrived in Los Angeles, Knight and his family arrived also, and for over a month the entire Brough family was together. Following the departure of Hillman and Anne, and Knight and family, Captain Brough wrote Anne a long letter which indicates that the get-together was a pleasant one.[33]

Unhappily, the good times of the summer, as recalled by the elder Brough, were followed a few months later by sorrow when Ruth, his daughter (Hillman and Knight's half-sister), died at the age of eighteen. There are no records to indicate whether Dr. Brough traveled to Los Angeles for the funeral; indeed, there is no evidence that he ever saw his father again prior to the latter's death in November 1910. The Brough-Roark scrapbook contains only one comment by the son regarding his father's death—a telegram from Los Angeles, indicating his stepmother was "bearing up well" and expressing appreciation for telegrams of sympathy from Anne, the "University boys," and others. A codicil to Captain Brough's will bequeathed a variety of possessions to Hillman Brough, including a diamond shirt stud, a scrapbook, a gold watch, and a silver napkin ring. Whether a more substantial legacy went to Hillman is not known.[34]

Dr. Brough and his wife lived in a white frame house which they had built on College Avenue, near the Baptist church. A picture of the home appears in the Brough-Roark scrapbook; it looks spacious and comfortable, and according to items in the society section of the Fayetteville newspaper, it was a lovely home "in its artistic and handsome furnishing, and air of culture lent by the presence of many books." The professor's financial circumstances are a matter of speculation; his salary at the university was modest—$2,200 for

1911–12—but he supplemented it with fees received for summer lyceum and chautauqua lectures. A brochure issued around 1909 promoted Brough as an outstanding orator who had spoken in many a "nook and hamlet." He delivered an average of about twenty-five commencement addresses per year and continued to be in demand by religious and fraternal organizations. How much compensation, if any, he received for his various speaking engagements is not known.[35]

Society news informs us that the Broughs frequently entertained friends in their home. The *Fayetteville Daily Democrat* reported on a series of small, informal evening parties at which the guests played progressive rook and hearts. One such party comprised eleven tables of players. Anne Brough also entertained with afternoon parties exclusively for ladies. In reporting on one such gathering, the newspaper noted that Mrs. Brough had "achieved so many successes this season that the most superlative degree of praise could scarcely do her justice." On occasion the Broughs also invited university students into their home, and apparently the professor and his wife were quite popular, both in the community and among the collegians.[36]

CHAPTER 3

The Professor in Politics

BEFORE TRACING DR. BROUGH's entry into Arkansas politics, a brief survey of the political climate in the early twentieth century will provide perspective on this turning point in the professor's career. Nationally, this period was the "era of progressivism"—a time of wide-ranging reform activity, bearing some resemblance to the populism and agrarian democracy of the nineties, but characterized by greater concerns for the problems of urban society. Leaders of progressive reform efforts, while sharing populistic goals in areas such as curbing corporate power and expanding democracy, differed from the more rural-oriented reformers in their emphasis on social justice, efficiency, and educational reform. Spokesmen for progressivism came from a variety of urban, middle-class people, including not only political leaders, but also educators, social workers, scholars, clergymen, businessmen, and newspaper editors and reporters. Of the latter, the so-called "muckrakers" were especially effective in calling attention to political, economic, and social problems of the modern, industrial age. Many progressive leaders, most notably Presidents Theodore Roosevelt and Woodrow Wilson, stood for an infusion of morality into politics.

For many years historians tended to ignore the South in their studies of progressivism; however, Prof. Arthur S. Link in a 1946 article clearly established the reality of a southern progressive movement in the late nineteenth and early twentieth centuries. More recently Prof. Dewey Grantham produced a thorough and lengthy examination of the region's participation in the reform movements of the progressive era. One of the "categories" of reform described by Grantham is "social control and state regulation," which furnishes useful insight into certain paradoxes in southern progressivism. The "social control" aspect was of especial importance with respect to race relations. Throughout the South successful steps were taken to disfranchise black citizens and impose a system of rigid racial segregation. Leaders of the dominant Democratic party saw these developments as essential to the achievement of a "white consensus" on the race question. This consensus was in turn necessary as a means of reducing factionalism within the party and enabling it to deal more effectively with "real" issues, including a variety of reforms. Other examples of "social control" and state regulation include penal reform, antimonopoly laws, legislation to regulate railroads, and prohibition. Grantham's study identifies other categories of southern progressivism, including social justice, educational reform, the quest for efficiency, and the broadening of democracy.[1]

Grantham and other scholars have examined the roles of a number of southern governors in the upsurge of progressivism in the early twentieth century. The administration of James K. Vardaman of Mississippi produced increased appropriations for public schools, higher salaries for teachers, and regulation of railroads, insurance companies, and banks. Gov. Richard I. Manning of South Carolina revised the state's taxing system and expanded state educational and social services. Sidney J. Catts of Florida supported labor unions (unusual for southern governors in this era), public health programs, penal reform, and increased spending for schools. Virginia's Westmoreland Davis, a "progressive insurgent," did battle with the party machine, supported prohibition, and established a more centralized and efficient administration, emulating modern business corporations. In North Carolina, Gov. Thomas W. Bickett emphasized better schools and roads and supported restrictions on child labor, as well as penal and welfare reform. Tennessee's Ben Walter Hooper, a Republican governor, secured reforms on behalf of education, labor, and prisoner welfare. Other progressive governors included Alabama's Braxton Bragg Comer and Kentucky's James McCrary.[2]

Antitrust laws and the regulation of railroads were the main themes in Arkansas progressivism at the turn of the century—along with the establishment of the white consensus and Democratic party ascendancy. The issue of curbing big business was the key to the initial political successes of Jeff Davis, who was elected governor in 1900 and re-elected in 1902 and 1904 to become Arkansas's first three-term governor. In the gubernatorial campaign of 1900 Davis pressed the need to enforce the state's antitrust law, which was his primary concern as attorney general. During his three terms Davis won much support from the "One-Gallus Democracy" of the countryside as he flailed the trusts, the railroads, Yankees, the "high-collared" city aristocrats, and the newspapers. His successful campaigns demonstrate the residual strength of agrarian radicalism and the effectiveness of his grass-roots political style.[3]

Soon after Davis's departure from the state house the complexion of Arkansas progressivism changed somewhat. The movement came increasingly under the influence of the middle class, which, despite its anxiety over the power of trusts and railroads, wished to implement certain reforms without antagonizing business and jeopardizing chances of attracting outside capital for economic development. Many middle-class citizens, including businessmen, clergymen, social workers, and educators, supported George W. Donaghey, a self-made businessman from Conway, in his campaign for governor. During and after his two terms (1909–1913), a flurry of reform activity occurred—for example, in the areas of educational reform and social justice. While such reforms were by no means neglected in the previous years, they received considerably more attention during Donaghey's terms and afterward.[4]

One of Donaghey's principal interests was education, an area in which Arkansas was seriously deficient. In 1910 the Southern Education Board, an adjunct of a major Rockefeller philanthropy, held its annual conference in Little Rock. In addition to generating publicity on Arkansas's educational problems, the board financed the work of a special commission to study these problems and make recommendations for their correction. The commission, whose members were appointed by Donaghey, made several recommendations based on its investigations, and in 1911 the general assembly followed some of these. Laws were enacted creating a state board of education, permitting consolidation of school districts, and authorizing state financial aid to the high schools. Donaghey's most spectacular action for reform was the blow he struck at the convict lease system. This system, by which contractors, railroad companies, and planters paid the state for the use of prisoners' labor, was a scandalous practice in several states. After reviewing reports of deplorable, often inhuman treatment of the convicts in prison camps, Donaghey urged the general assembly to abolish the system. When this was not done, the governor in 1912 chose a dramatic way to focus both state and national attention on the problem: he pardoned 360 convicts. Following Donaghey's tenure as governor the general assembly passed legislation terminating the lease system. Donaghey was also a sympathetic observer of developments in social welfare, and it was during his term that the state conference of charities and correction was created and held its first meeting in Little Rock. Membership in this conference included not only social workers, but also clergymen, doctors, businessmen, and educators.[5]

In Fayetteville, Dr. Brough was interested in and supportive of much of the Arkansas progressive agenda, as evidenced in some of his addresses to various groups. He delivered a speech at Sulfur Springs in 1909 in which he pointed out that Arkansas's average number of school days per year was 90.2, as compared with the national average of 144, and in various addresses advocated a special millage tax for support of the university. In other speeches he urged greater financial aid from the state for both the schools and the university, called for a campaign against illiteracy, paid tribute to women for their contributions to the betterment of society, and supported various "social justice" causes. Brough, like other progressive-minded citizens, was supportive of state and regional efforts at uplift and reform. In 1912 he attended the first meeting of the Southern Sociological Congress at Nashville and was appointed as one of the organization's directors. The congress was committed to various social reforms, in such areas as prison conditions, public health, child welfare, and race relations. At its first meeting the Congress identified a number of challenges for southern white society—including a call to "prove its superior civilization by a greater degree of kindness and justice to an inferior race." Brough was named chairman of a university committee which was charged with studying and reporting on the "Southern Race Question." The report of the commission, which Brough prepared, retained the paternalistic tone of the congress's "challenge." It rejected the concept of social equality, yet asserted that the Negro should be assured basic rights of life, liberty, and the pursuit of happiness.[6]

According to Robert Leflar, Dr. Brough's political ambitions were well known to his colleagues as early as 1909. In his history of the University of Arkansas, Leflar recounts a conversation among several university professors, including Brough, following an address by William Jennings Bryan in a Fayetteville church. After Bryan left, Brough began praising him as America's greatest orator. Another professor told him, "You'll be governor, yet, Brough, just keep it up. We're all for you." Some of Brough's students at the university even addressed him as "Governor." His enormous popularity as a teacher resulted in the formation of a loyal group of future political partisans who eventually worked zealously for him in his political campaigns.[7]

Holding a faculty position at a university was not necessarily an asset in running for political office, but the elevation of the southern-born Democrat, Woodrow Wilson, to the presidency in 1912 showed that a career in academe did not preclude success in politics. Wilson had been a professor and a university president before entering New Jersey politics in 1910. His victory in the presidential contest elated southerners; for the first time since Andrew Johnson a southern-born man was occupying the White House. In the opinion of many Arkansans, Wilson's career might be paralleled in Arkansas if Dr. Brough were to become governor. There was a growing dissatisfaction with

the "same old gang" of political leaders in the state, and many citizens probably thought that a leader who was *not* a professional politician—particularly
one who was erudite, articulate, and of impeccable integrity—would be a welcome change. A Mississippi friend, upon learning that Brough was contem-
plating a race for governor in 1913, wrote him as follows:

> It is pleasing to know that such men of your intellectuality are forging to the
> front as a result of the progressive ideas that are in the ascendancy now; and
> to know that the old political croakers who predicted that the movement for
> more power to the people meant elevation of politicians and demagogues ...
> were grossly ignorant of the intelligence of the masses.[8]

There were certain obvious parallels between the careers of Wilson and
Brough, although Wilson's achievements as both a scholar and a politician
greatly outshone those of the Arkansas professor. Both had Ph.D.'s from Johns
Hopkins; both had spent many years in the classroom; both placed much
emphasis on the importance of moral values. Brough was one of Wilson's
foremost fans in Arkansas, and claimed to have started the first "Wilson for
President" club in the South. He also said that he was one of Wilson's students
at Hopkins—not quite an accurate statement, for Brough was simply a member of the audience when Wilson came to the campus periodically as a guest
lecturer.[9]

Brough's initial venture into politics was tentative and short-lived. In 1913
he announced his candidacy for the unexpired term of Gov. Joseph T. (Joe)
Robinson, whom the legislature had chosen to fill a vacancy in the United
States Senate. Upon hearing of Brough's announcement, many of his followers
expressed elation and optimism; some of them pointed to the fact that
Arkansas, like the nation, was about to have a "scholar in politics" for its
leader. One supporter predicted that Dr. Brough, if elected, would provide
the most intellectual and progressive leadership in the state's history. There
were other enthusiastic responses to his candidacy·

> We need statesmen instead of politicians in our public offices. ... When such
> men as honorable Woodrow Wilson and Dr. Charles Hillman Brough are put
> forward by the people for political preferment then the country is surely com-
> ing into its own.

> You will have an opportunity to be of great assistance to a state just becom-
> ing conscious of its full duty to the future.

> Arkansas needs men of decision, of character, economic training who thor-
> oughly understand the science of good government.[10]

Despite these and other sanguine comments from loyal former students and others, Brough suddenly withdrew from the 1913 campaign, explaining that the brief time allotted for the special election was insufficient for a thorough discussion of the issues. Another reason he gave for his withdrawal was his belief that if he stayed in the race he would be obliged to resign his position at the university, ". . . so as not to involve this splendid institution of higher learning in politics in any way." In 1915 Brough decided the times were more propitious for him to seek the governorship, so he resigned from the university faculty and began planning for the Democratic primary to be held in the spring of 1916. An editorial in the *Fort Smith Times Record* applauded Brough's sense of propriety in refusing to remain on the state payroll while running for office, and observed that there were many politicians who were not bothered by such scruples. Brough resigned his job effective July 1, 1915. "For this rift in the dark clouds of Arkansas politics," said the editorial writer, "we are truly grateful." Brough's candidacy in 1916 was especially attractive to middle-class Arkansans who were urban oriented and business minded. Many of these people were disturbed by the radical rhetoric of reformers like Jeff Davis, who represented an attack on middle-class values and a rabble-rousing political style. These middle-class citizens tended to favor the more moderate progressivism of George W. Donaghey, and they perceived Brough as a proponent of the same moderate approach to reform.[11]

Brough's candidacy did not open officially until 1916, but his busy speaking schedule kept him in the public eye as he traveled throughout the state in 1914 and 1915, and continued to impress potential voters. He accelerated his speaking activities in the spring of 1915, delivering eighteen speeches in an eight-hour period in June. He was a candidate in every way but name, and long before the formal launching of his campaign for the Democratic nomination, many of his friends were pledging their loyalty, offering advice on political strategy, and volunteering to campaign for him. Their exuberant praise for Brough was essentially the same response which his 1913 sortie had produced. Former University of Arkansas students were among his most enthusiastic well-wishers; these, and many of the students who were still enrolled at the university, enlisted the aid of their parents on behalf of Dr. Brough. Students also sent him lists of voters' names and addresses, and worked at canvassing their communities, promoting his candidacy. "Brough Clubs" sprang up in a number of communities. One of the earliest of these, not surprisingly, was formed at the university; in June 1915 about two hundred students met and organized for the purpose of getting every student and former student of the University of Arkansas to pledge support for Dr. Brough either by active work or with financial contributions. Many of his supporters were middle-class business and professional people, although not necessarily from large towns. Supporters who wrote encouraging letters included a Lewisville lawyer, an Elks Club officer, a court stenographer, and the mayor of De Queen. Brough's plan to enter the 1916 primary had a large impact on the educational community as well. A Benton County teachers' association adopted a resolution endorsing Brough, "the Woodrow Wilson of Arkansas," and suggested that he could liberate Arkansas from the professional politicians and place the state

> upon that plane of honor and administrative efficiency to which she naturally belongs, with the welfare of the whole people her first consideration, and personal ambition in the background.

A teachers' institute in Craighead County passed a resolution which said they "would be rejoiced to see such an able and excellent gentleman, from their own ranks, at the helm of the Government of our State."[12]

Brough's campaign platform was well developed by the fall of 1915, and it included a number of progressive objectives. He promised support of legislation for the betterment of the schools, colleges, and the state university; he called for the enactment of a primary election law designed to ensure honesty at the polls; he pledged to enforce the recently enacted statewide prohibition law; and he promised to introduce greater economy and efficiency in the administration of state government. This agenda was representative of the "business progressivism" advocated by many middle-class citizens who wished to promote a moderate program of reform while at the same time bring about the application of businesslike methods in the management of state affairs. The need for more efficient and economical administration was a recurring theme in Brough's campaign speeches, whether he was discussing tax assessment, education, economic growth, or management of state institutions. Consistent with the goal of efficiency was Brough's call for improvements in transportation, especially the building of good roads. He noted that the Arkansas farmer had to pay 26.8 cents to haul one ton one mile to market, as compared with about eight cents for farmers living in states with good roads.[13]

Brough's rivals for the Democratic nomination for governor were T. C. McRae, Earle W. Hodges, and L. C. Smith. McRae was a former congressman who had retired to practice law in Prescott; Hodges was secretary of state and an experienced Arkansas politician who reportedly controlled the political "machinery" of the state; Smith, a former county judge, was believed to have the backing of the liquor interests. McRae withdrew from the primary race early in January 1916.[14]

Brough and his followers regarded Hodges as a more formidable opponent than Smith, and the Hodges forces viewed Dr. Brough in the same manner. Hodges attempted to discredit Brough with a number of charges which were unrelated to the latter's campaign platform; he asserted that Brough was not a true southerner, that he was a Mormon and a Negrophile, that his father was a "carpetbagger," and that the university professor was "too intellectual" and thus likely to be out of touch with the ordinary Arkansas citizen.[15]

In view of Brough's numerous speeches in praise of the South (both "Old" and "New") and its heroes, there would seem to be no doubt of his attachment to the region. Nevertheless, Brough went to considerable effort to assure voters that he definitely was a southerner. At his request, Sen. John Williams and Rep. W. W. Venable of Mississippi wrote letters attesting to his Mississippi origins:

> [Williams]: I have no doubt of the fact that you were born in Mississippi upon the date that you give.
> [Venable]: I have known you and your family all my life, and I know it to be a fact that you were born in Clinton, Mississippi. . . .

Venable further testified that Brough's father lived in Utah during Reconstruction and played no part in "carpet-bag rule." A more extensive statement affirming Brough's affinity for the South was provided by Rev. B. R. Womack, who had twice served as pastor of the Russellville Baptist church. The Reverend Mr. Womack, who had achieved prominence as an editor, college professor, and college president, denounced Hodges' "low and disgraceful appeal to sectionalism," and described Dr. Brough as a man who

> fed on the products of the South, . . . breathed the atmosphere of the South, . . . imbibed the spirit of the people of the South, . . . grew up in the society of the South, . . . learned to love the men and the institutions of the South, . . . received all the education that could be given him in the South, and . . . has devoted his splendid talents, without reserve, to the best interests and advancements of the South . . .

An ex-president of Blue Mountain College (Mississippi) wrote that Brough had "always been a true and patriotic southerner," and that the Hillmans "were two of Mississippi's greatest educators and greatest citizens." Whether Brough had these testimonies duplicated and distributed to voters, or merely cited them in his speeches, is not known.[16]

Hodges' campaign literature claimed that Brough was not only a member of the Latter-day Saints' church, but was a Mormon elder and had taught in a Mormon college. This charge was easily refuted, for Brough was widely known as a leader in the Baptist church; in fact, he was a senior deacon in the church at Fayetteville. He pointed out that his only "connection" with the Mormons was his study of their irrigation activities in Utah. In labeling Brough a "Negrophile" the Hodges forces were attempting to show that Brough, as chairman of the Southern Sociological Congress' University Race Commission, had adopted a liberal view of race relations. Brough had indeed chaired that commission, and had also given a speech on the southern race problem in December 1914 at Washington, D.C. In response to his opponents' charges of "liberalism" on the issue, he explained that he had been appointed commission chairman by Dr. James H. Dillard, a "native Southern rock-ribbed Democrat," and that both the commission report and the Washington speech had adhered to the southern viewpoint of opposition to social equality of the Negro with whites. Moreover, Brough issued a statement expressing his opposition to social equality between the races and to negroes serving on juries. He also obtained testimonies (as in the case of the "Southern" issue) to demonstrate that he was "safe" on the race question. One testimony stated that Brough's upbringing was such as to "absolutely preclude the possibility of his imbibing any sentiment on the Negro question except those held by the pure type of southern men and women formed at a time when the lines of discrimination were rigidly drawn." Brough himself responded to the Negrophile charge:

> We know and appreciate the fact that the Negro is with us to stay ... His very existence in our midst creates a problem with which we must deal, whether we would or not. As to how this question is to be dealt with, I know of no better way than by encouraging them to improve their race—mentally, that they may understand the right, and, morally, that they may be able to do it.[17]

Hodges' appeal to the anti-intellectual element, by characterizing the professor as too educated for Arkansas citizens, may have repelled as many voters as it attracted. Evidently many citizens were pleased at the prospect of having a governor who would be a symbol of respectability and progress and who would help dispel the widely held image of Arkansas as a backward and primitive province. Some supporters of Brough believed that as governor he would prove to be an excellent "advertisement" for Arkansas. Brough himself was well aware of the state's negative image and was convinced that it was undeserved, springing primarily from such sources as Thomas Jackson's jokebook, *On a Slow Train through Arkansaw.* He believed Arkansas, like the "New South," had made great strides, both economically and culturally.[18]

Except for asserting his commitment to better roads for Arkansas, Brough had little in his platform in 1916 that specifically focused on the economic needs of farmers, although his clearly stated support for statewide prohibition and his reputation as a staunch Baptist appealed to rural and small-town citizens throughout the state. As for the labor vote, Brough seems to have secured it by promising to "favor union labor," a commitment which won the public endorsement of the president of the Arkansas Federation of Labor. Brough's advocacy of the eight-hour day for railroad workers also helped attract votes from that group; according to a railway conductor, thousands of votes were assured for the professor by a speech in favor of that measure, delivered at Argenta two days before the primary election.[19]

Apparently many Arkansas voters were convinced that the incumbent governor, George W. Hays, and his allies, were intimately allied with the St. Francis Levee District Board, whose "machine politics" allegedly manipulated votes in eastern Arkansas to ensure Hays's victory over his opponent in the 1913 Democratic primary. The returns in that primary were contested, but the party's state central committee ruled in favor of Hays. Observing the factionalism within the Democratic party, some Republicans were optimistic about their chances in the July general election; however, the Democratic nominee easily won that race, as was usual in that era of one-party domination in Arkansas. Suspicions of Hays's indebtedness to the "machine" increased when, as governor, he declined to support reform legislation which would make membership on the Levee Board elective rather than appointive.[20]

Although Hays did not seek renomination in 1916, Brough and his supporters believed that the incumbent and his machine had formed a close alliance with Hodges for the purpose of perpetuating the machine's power. Thus the Brough campaign (in speeches, fliers, etc.) focused much attention on the "Hays-Hodges Combine." In one address Brough charged that the governor's office was a "clearing house for the Hodges campaign," and proceeded to castigate Hays at great length, painting him as a "small politician" surrounded by a "little coterie of office seekers." Brough continued by indicting the governor of many specific improprieties and told his audience that this record of malfeasance clearly showed that Hays was a machine politician and that a victory for Hodges would ensure continued control by the machine. Brough emphasized that it was time for the office of governor to cease to be the headquarters for machine politics and the guardian of that system. He pledged a different policy if he were elected:

> The affairs of this state will be run in broad daylight, and . . . the activity of the "ward politician" in state affairs . . . shall be only a hideous memory.[21]

Reluctantly accepting the advice of some of his campaign advisers, Brough added a number of eastern Arkansas counties to his speechmaking itinerary. Although this was considered to be an area of strength for Hodges—where machine politics was so entrenched—the tour by Brough was effective, resulting in a victory for him in every county in which he spoke. While Brough and Hodges were laboring to discredit each other, L. C. Smith, the third candidate for the Democratic nomination, ran a quiet campaign and hoped his two rivals would extirpate each other. When the vote count in the March 29 primary was completed, Smith had a slightly larger total than Hodges—34,918 to 32,292. However, Brough had won a convincing 48,892 votes, and since there was no run-off provision, his plurality gave him the Democratic nomination. Brough carried Pulaski County, east Arkansas, and the hill counties; Smith's votes came mainly from south Arkansas; and Hodges' support was scattered widely over the state. Winning the Democratic primary was tantamount to being elected governor; and Brough easily defeated his opponents in the general election in November, receiving 122,041 votes to 43,963 for the Republican candidate and 9,730 for the Socialist.[22]

CHAPTER 4

A Progressive Governor

D URING HIS FIRST TERM, Gov. Charles Hillman Brough, in the words of one scholar, "caught Progressivism at high tide," a few years after its acceptability had been established by Governor Donaghey. The "professor in politics" was thus able to secure a host of progressive measures during the 1917 legislative session. However, after the United States joined in the war against Germany, Brough's domestic agenda received less attention as he devoted much of his time and energy in support of the war effort.[1]

The Broughs' jubilation over the victory in the general election was marred in late December when a fire destroyed their home on College Avenue in Fayetteville. No one was injured in the blaze, but Dr. Brough estimated the loss to be around $2,500 to $3,000 above insurance. In addition, members of the Cabeen family, who were house guests of the Broughs, suffered personal property loss of about $500. Among the condolences was a letter from Rev. Sam H. Campbell, pastor of the Second Baptist Church in Little Rock, whose expression of sorrow at the Broughs' loss was coupled with a lengthy invitation to join Campbell's church when they moved to the capital city. They subsequently accepted the invitation.[2]

Early in January Mrs. Brough was the guest of honor at a number of parties and receptions, including an open house at the Twentieth Century Club. The organization broke from its tradition of honoring departing members with a members-only luncheon; since the wife of the governor-elect "belonged more or less to everybody," the club published a general invitation in the social columns of the *Fayetteville Daily Democrat*.[3]

Shortly before leaving Fayetteville the governor-elect and his wife were honored by the First Baptist Church in a special farewell service. At the service the pastor, Dr. L. E. Barton, presented them with a silver loving cup, "appropriately inscribed," and brief laudatory addresses were given by several members of the congregation. Three of the talks extolled Dr. Brough as teacher, statesman, and Christian. The fourth, titled "Dr. Brough's Partner, Mrs. Brough," recounted Anne's involvement in the social, educational, and cultural life of the community, in addition to church work.[4]

The new governor received numerous congratulatory messages, many of them reflecting confidence that his administration would be a progressive one. And soon after the Broughs moved to Little Rock, the Arkansas Elks presented the governor—who was a member—with a "fine touring car," along with an auto license, a gasoline coupon book, and a leather-bound roster of all the lodges participating in the gift. In addition to enjoying broad support and good wishes from ardent supporters, the new governor was even able to secure the good will of his erstwhile adversary, Earle Hodges. Early in Brough's administration, Hodges issued a statement commending Brough for doing a good job. Hodges said he was almost sorry he tried to beat him! In response, the governor expressed gratitude to his former rival for the support he had given to some progressive measures Brough had proposed to the legislature. In addition to putting aside his differences with Hodges, Brough showed his ability to rise above politics by persuading the state senate to receive officially a list of recess appointments made by Governor Hays. A Texarkana newspaper viewed this as placing the new administration on a "high plane."[5]

The educator-turned-governor was practically bald and had sparkling eyes and a prominent Roman nose. He had "fleshened out" considerably since his Clinton years, and his ears no longer looked over-sized. He was clean shaven, having abandoned the mustache of his youth. Although a man of commanding appearance, at five feet ten inches, the dignified, professorial mien was balanced by a gregarious, down-to-earth manner. Despite his erudition and oratorical ability, he was "simple and human in all his inclinations."[6]

Brough's inaugural speech to the Forty-First General Assembly, some twenty-seven thousand words long, was perhaps the longest inaugural address in the state's history. Had the speech been delivered in its entirety, at one hundred words per minute, it would have lasted four and one-half hours; however, the governor probably read only the title captions of many subjects.[7]

In his message Brough pledged a "safe and sane business administration," based on efficiency, and assured the lawmakers that under his leadership the statehouse would not be "a laboratory for experiment with political theories. . . ." Nonetheless, the governor's address called for enactment of what must have been considered a progressive program: greater support for education, placing the state on a "cash basis," reforms in the area of charities and correction, woman suffrage, creation of a new constitution, construction of a state-supported system of paved roads, and prohibition. Following the legislative session, the *Arkansas Gazette* described it as the most constructive in the state's history. About seven-eighths of the governor's program was enacted into law. Even Brough's most outspoken opponents agreed that the governor had skillfully steered the legislation; usually a message from him proved sufficient to secure passage of a bill. Most of the progressive measures passed during Brough's administration were the work of the 1917 session (although some such laws were passed by the 1919 legislature and by special sessions). The following discussion of progressive accomplishments focuses primarily on the 1917 legislative session.[8]

Educational progress had high priority with the governor, and it was apparent that his commitment to this goal was widely applauded and supported by the electorate. His victories in the 1916 primary and general election were indicative of their support of education; and another sign of this was their approval of Amendment Twelve to the state constitution, which raised the limit of local taxation for educational purposes. The amendment had been vigorously promoted by the state teachers' association and had also been endorsed by the Democratic party platform, which was drafted by Brough.[9]

In his inaugural speech the new governor proposed that the legislature of 1917 adopt laws which would further strengthen public schools and higher education. One reform Brough sought was a measure to place the state educational institutions on a millage basis. This was designed to relieve the institutions from the need to engage in biennial "politicking" with the legislators. In urging the lawmakers of 1917 to enact the measure, Brough predicted that if the institutions of higher learning—"the capstone of our educational system—are not properly supported, the youth of Arkansas would likely leave the state to attend college, thus weakening their link with the state." The legislature responded by adopting this reform and in addition enacted several other education measures, including the following: (1) the compulsory attendance law, which required that after September 1, 1917, all children aged seven to fifteen must attend school, and that each student attend at least three-fourths of the session; (2) the textbook uniformity law, which established statewide adoption, a plan which progressive-minded leaders believed to be both economical and efficient; (3) creation of a state illiteracy commission; and (4) legislation accepting federal aid for vocational education through the Smith-Lever Act and providing for the teaching of agriculture in the rural high schools. Following adjournment of the legislature of 1917, Brough in an address to the state teachers' association commended the lawmakers for passing "more legislation of a constructive nature along educational lines, than at any other period in Arkansas's history."[10]

Brough's progressive agenda also included proposals regarding the state's fiscal condition. The most pressing problems were the deficit and a poor credit standing. In his inaugural address Brough urged the legislature to approve a note issue to pay off the existing debt and a revenue plan to place Arkansas on a cash basis. The lawmakers approved this as well as several other recommendations by the governor in the area of taxation, all of which were consistent with the goal of efficiency in state government.[11]

A number of items in Brough's program of reform concerned state responsibilities in charities and corrections. He had been actively involved in the work of the Southern Sociological Congress and was sympathetic with the "social justice" goals of that organization, as well as those of the Arkansas Conference on Charities and Correction. For example, the governor supported the Arkansas conference's proposal for the creation of a state commission on charities and correction, to be "charged with the oversight and study and improvement of the institutional life of the State, public and private." This proposal, which the legislature adopted, was backed not only by the state conference, but also by the Farmers' Union, the State Federation of Labor, and the Arkansas Federation of Women's Clubs. The functions of the new commission included assisting private charitable agencies in standardizing their work, supervising juvenile court work, and promoting parole work for the industrial schools.[12]

The industrial schools represent another facet of the social justice movement. A state reform school for boys had been established in Little Rock in 1905, and with the Juvenile Court Act of 1911 reflected the modern trend toward providing special treatment for youthful delinquents. However, there was no state-supported institution for delinquent girls until the legislature in 1917 followed the recommendations of Brough and the social work forces and established a Girls' Industrial School. The same act provided that the new institution use the buildings of the boys' reform school, which was in turn removed to a different location. Additional reforms of the social justice variety in 1917 included a modest program of financial assistance for mothers with dependent children ("mothers' pensions"—the forerunner of aid-to-dependent-children programs).[13]

Like many progressive politicians Brough was committed to the broadening of democracy. For example, he supported a more "direct democracy" in the form of the initiative and referendum. This reform had been instituted as the Tenth Amendment to the state constitution, largely through the efforts of Governor Donaghey—with vital help from William Jennings Bryan, who stumped the state on behalf of the amendment. In the years preceding Brough's election, however, supreme court rulings had greatly reduced the effectiveness of the initiative and referendum, and in 1916 a new proposal, Amendment 13, was devised as a means of strengthening the process. Candidate Brough endorsed the proposal, and was disappointed at its failure of adoption in the fall election.[14]

Brough also favored the extension of the suffrage to women, and expressed this view during his campaign for the primary nomination in 1916. However, this reform was not included among the major recommendations to the legislature in his 1917 inaugural speech; he touched only fleetingly on the subject in a paragraph listing reforms he believed should be incorporated in a new state constitution. But the governor, when given the opportunity during the 1917 legislative session, did lend his influence on behalf of the suffragist cause. The movement in Arkansas had lagged in the early years of the new century, but had gained momentum in the period 1911–17. One of the principal arguments favoring the ballot for women was that they needed it as a means of working more effectively in the cause of social reform. Opponents of woman suffrage maintained that women should not dabble in the "men's world" of politics but should confine their interests and activities mainly to the "domestic sphere." After failing to get a suffrage amendment to the state constitution before the people in 1915, the suffragists concentrated on a more limited goal: the right to vote in Arkansas primary elections. This could be achieved through an act of the legislature, whereas full suffrage required a constitutional amendment.[15]

During the first week of March 1917, suffragist leaders were apparently confident of their prospects of gaining the primary elections ballot, for they conducted a "suffrage school" at the Little Rock Public Library, under the auspices of the National American Woman Suffrage Association. The women in charge of the school—in which more than one hundred women enrolled—were Mrs. T. T. Cotnam of Little Rock, Miss Annie Doughty of New York, and Mrs. Halsey W. Wilson of New Jersey. Mrs. Cotnam had the distinction of being the first woman to address the Arkansas General Assembly on behalf of woman suffrage.[16]

Although he was not in the forefront of the effort to secure the primary vote for women, Governor Brough was sympathetic to the reform, and was delighted to sign the bill which received legislative approval on March 7. The elated suffragists and their allies staged a victory celebration which included a mass meeting at the Marion Hotel; the meeting room was crowded to overflowing. The featured speaker was Brough, who delivered a stirring address prior to signing the bill. The governor said he shared the "pardonable pride" of those who had fought for woman suffrage through the years and asserted his belief that

> woman suffrage will be a mighty factor in the educational, social, and moral amelioration of our state.

Brough's support rested largely on his recognition of the important role played by women in various progressive causes, such as those promoted by women's clubs, the state conference on charities and correction, and the Southern Sociological Congress. In an address to the Arkansas Federation of Women's Clubs (in which Mrs. Brough was active), Brough paid tribute to "the ladies of the Federation, [who] by their concerted efforts, have ushered in a new progress era in their various states. . . ."[17]

The governor expected full suffrage for women to be obtained as one of the reforms in a proposed new state constitution. In his inaugural address he characterized the existing constitution, created in the aftermath of Radical Reconstruction, as inadequate for modern times. He pointed out the need for a new constitution which would provide broader powers for government and longer terms for officials. The lawmakers responded by approving a bill to hold a constitutional convention, but the votes—53 to 46 in the House and 21 to 14 in the Senate—hardly indicated overwhelming support for the measure.[18]

One of Brough's major goals was the creation of a state-supported system of paved roads which would increase the economic efficiency of both agriculture and business. An enthusiastic leader of the good roads movement, and a leader in the United States Good Roads Association, Brough actually wished to see not only a comprehensive road system for Arkansas, but the development of an interstate highway network. In his campaign speeches and in his inaugural address of 1917 the governor made several recommendations for legislative action on roadbuilding. He urged generous appropriations for that purpose and called attention to the fact that federal matching funds were available under the recently enacted Federal Aid Road Act. Brough also proposed the creation of an advisory board to supervise road construction and that work on the roads be done by state convicts. The governor's proposals were favorably received by the legislature during Brough's terms in office; the 1919 legislature was particularly responsive to the growing demand for road

improvement, passing hundreds of bills to establish local road-building districts. Although the result was hardly the efficient, comprehensive system the
governor had envisioned, he applauded the actions of the lawmakers as "progressive." A similar assessment was given in an article in the *Arkansas Gazette*
Centennial Supplement, which predicted that completion of the projected
road construction would put an end to the state's backwoods status:

> Our state, thrown open to the public at last, with its splendid climate, rich
> soil, and wonderful natural resources, will become a leader among the States
> of the Union.[19]

Prohibition of liquor was among the topics Brough addressed in his 1917
inaugural speech, expressing satisfaction at the progress of that reform but
calling on the lawmakers to take additional steps to curb "demon rum" in
Arkansas. The previous legislature had enacted a statewide "bone dry" law,
which prohibited further issuance of licenses to sell, make, or give away liquor
after January 1, 1916. The liquor forces tried to restore "local option" through
an initiated act in 1916, but the voters soundly defeated that attempt in the
November election. (This effort by the liquor interests to take advantage of
"direct democracy" produced considerable apprehension among Arkansas
prohibition advocates and led many of them to oppose Amendment 13, which
was designed to revise and strengthen the initiative and referendum.) At the
governor's urging, the 1917 legislature enacted a new, tougher "bone dry"
measure which prohibited shipments of liquor into the state. The sentiment
for prohibition increased, in Arkansas and in many other states, as a result
of American entry into World War I; Brough and others pointed out, for
example, that the war effort demanded using grain to produce food rather
than liquor. The proposed new constitution contained a provision which
would have fixed statewide prohibition in a more secure status. Although the
voters rejected that document in December 1918, Arkansas remained dry under
existing state law, and in 1919 the ratification of the Eighteenth Amendment
theoretically placed the entire nation in that condition. Arkansas was the
twenty-seventh state to approve the prohibition amendment, with only two
dissenting votes in the House of Representatives and none in the Senate.[20]

Brough's chief adversary in the May 1918 Democratic primary was L. C.
"Judge" Smith, who was said to favor the repeal of Arkansas's prohibition law.
Brough won a decisive victory over Smith, and in the general election tri-
umphed with a landslide over the Socialist candidate; the Republicans
declined to nominate a candidate to oppose the governor in 1918. In the primary, the Smith forces claimed that Brough, who was receiving a lot of press

coverage of his activities for the war effort, was using the "cloak of patriotism" to gain votes. Whether or not this charge was justified, it is true that the governor was devoting most of his time to urging his fellow Arkansans to rally behind the federal government's various "home front" programs—such as food and fuel conservation, Liberty Loan drives, and Red Cross work.[21]

Brough's oratorical skills were applied to the cause of patriotism; he delivered scores of inspirational speeches both in and outside of the state. Newspaper clippings in the family scrapbook attest to Brough's ability to stimulate patriotism; for example, a rousing speech at the Arkansas Bankers' Association banquet at Hot Springs brought the delegates to their feet, cheering and waving their napkins. And at a Liberty Loan rally at Hamburg, Brough spoke for an hour and a half, then presented honor medals to several local Boy Scouts, each of the boys saluting, and in turn being saluted by the governor. A 1918 handbill announced that Brough was to deliver five speeches on one day—at five different towns—on behalf of the war savings stamps campaign. He gave a number of patriotic speeches outside the state. Addressing a St. Louis audience, he asserted that there was "no twilight zone in American patriotism. In this war we are either for the president and for the flag, or we are against the president and against the flag." A Missouri newspaper applauded this sentiment, and contrasted the Arkansas governor's stalwart patriotism with the antiwar stand of Wisconsin's Senator LaFollette. Brough, in an address at Milwaukee, denounced LaFollette, labeling him a Bolshevik leader! Brough's anti-radicalism, both during and following the war, was the subject of a humorous skit by the Gridiron Club of Little Rock in 1919. The governor, who was the target of the group's "roast," was unable to attend. A performer in the skit read a letter supposedly written by Brough, explaining that he was busy crusading against the Bolsheviks. The reader closed the letter with a gentle slap at Brough's elaborate signature: "Yours all over the bottom of the page, Charles Hillman Brough."[22]

In setting a proper example for Arkansas citizens, Brough even planted a garden in 1918, raising radishes, lettuces, and beans. A news item pointed out that he could be seen early in the morning, in the yard at Arch and Twenty-First Street, working with hoe and rake. It was reported that Mrs. Brough was her husband's principal adviser, but that neighbors were not hesitant to offer their advice, also. The governor was ill for a brief period during the summer of 1918—whether from overexertion in the garden, or in his speechmaking and other efforts in support of the war, is not known. Following his recovery, he and Anne moved to a home at 1404 Scott Street, which had been occupied by Gov. Augustus H. Garland in the 1870s. In a letter to his nephew in Vicksburg

(Knight's son, Charlie), inviting him to visit, the governor described the house as having a big guest room, electric fans, and a pantry "filled with good preserves." Brough promised the youngster that they would talk about the war, President Wilson, and the Kaiser, and that the lad could run the governor's office during his visit.[23]

The chief war mobilization authority in the state was the Arkansas Council of Defense, which consisted of thirty-three citizens, mostly middle-class businessmen, appointed by Governor Brough in May 1917. The Arkansas Council was part of a nationwide network set up by the federal government, with each state council working immediately under the National Council of Defense. The Arkansas state council, along with local councils throughout the state, led citizens in support of various home front activities, such as Liberty Loan drives and Red Cross work. In addition, the Arkansas Council launched a campaign to curb venereal disease and issued publications on such problems as vagrancy and desertion from the army. Included on the state council was one female member, Mrs. Joseph Frauenthal of Conway, who led in the formation of a separate "Women's Committee of the Council of Defense for Arkansas." Prominent in this committee was Mrs. Brough, who served as its chairman. The Women's Committee aided significantly in Liberty Loan drives, and in addition worked with state home demonstration agents, helping to enlist girls and women to work in the production and conservation of food and in the strengthening of family health. As chairman of the Women's Committee Mrs. Brough supervised a Liberty Loan exhibit which featured captured German war paraphernalia.[24]

While the war effort commanded most of the governor's attention and energy in 1918—his renomination and re-election efforts were subordinated to that effort—he naturally maintained a keen interest in the work of the state constitutional convention. As noted earlier, the bill providing for a convention had met with considerable opposition in the 1917 legislature; and although the *Arkansas Gazette* and the state Bar Association were among the strong advocates for a new constitution, there were suspicious voices raised from the beginning. The *Arkansas Methodist*, for example, suspected that certain special interests, rather than the rank-and-file citizens, stood to benefit from the reform.[25]

Delegates to the convention were elected and convened in November 1917, but stayed in session only long enough to establish committees which were to prepare recommendations for the convention to consider when it reconvened in July 1918. Many of these recommendations were provisions which Brough wanted in the new constitution: four-year terms (e.g., for governor), women's suffrage, limitations on local legislation (by the state legislature), improvements in the initiative and referendum, and authorizations for city and county bond issues. (Of course, there were numerous other items covered in the document.) The governor's influence was considerable; in fact, many referred to the convention as the "Brough Convention." Prior to the election he delivered a number of speeches in favor of adoption, sometimes giving three speeches in one day. On election day, Saturday, December 14, the voter turnout was poor. Extremely cold weather in the northern parts of the state, flooding along the White and Black Rivers, and an influenza epidemic kept large numbers of eligible voters away from the polls. The 1918 constitution failed of adoption by about 13,000 votes. Reasons for its defeat, in addition to the pathetic voter turnout, included opposition among the small farmers in the hill counties who perceived the new constitution as being too identified with the wealthy landowners of the delta region. Crestfallen at the setback for reform, Brough tried to persuade the 1919 legislature to revise and resubmit the document, but the lawmakers declined to do so.[26]

Much of the work of the Forty-Second Assembly was road legislation— chiefly acts creating road improvement districts. There were so many of these measures that two large volumes of road acts were published in 1919, in addition to a volume containing general legislation and another for various special measures. The governor was gratified at the progress of the good roads campaign, but he had other items on his progressive agenda for 1919 as well. For example, he wished to salvage certain reforms contained in the defeated constitution. He urged ratification of a federal women's suffrage amendment, whenever Congress referred one to the legislatures; he also recommended submission of a woman suffrage amendment to the state constitution. Within a few days the legislature complied with the latter proposal by passing a resolution, which the governor signed. The ratification vote was to take place in the next general election (1920). The importance of this proposed amendment was greatly diminished by the ratification in 1920 of the federal woman suffrage amendment—the so-called "Susan B. Anthony" Amendment. Arkansas gave its approval by means of a joint resolution passed by a special session of the legislature called by Brough in late July 1919. Brough signed the resolution on July 30. Another reform contained in the 1918 constitution was the establishment of a state corporation commission to provide greater "State surveillance of all corporations and individuals engaged in public callings...." As he customarily did when advocating legislation, Brough pointed out that many other states—in this instance, forty—had already taken such action. The legislature complied and the commission was created, although

Brough's successor, Thomas C. McRae, persuaded the 1921 legislature to abolish it.[27]

Governor Brough asked the lawmakers to strengthen the state's prohibition law (this, too, had been written into the ill-fated document of 1918), and strongly recommended the ratification of the prohibition amendment to the federal Constitution.[28]

One of the items on the governor's progressive agenda involved some "unfinished business" in the area of corrections. The 1917 legislature had appropriated fifty thousand dollars for a Girls' Industrial School, but insufficient revenues obliged Brough to veto all of the appropriation except for the clause providing for maintenance of the school. However, federal funds combined with money contributed by Arkansas citizens made possible not only the Industrial School, but a state reformatory for women as well. During the war, Mrs. Martha B. Falconer, representing the federal government, made a study of the Camp Pike area and concluded that Arkansas ranked forty-sixth among the states in the care of delinquent girls and women. In her opinion, both an industrial school and a woman's reformatory were a war necessity. She offered to secure fifty thousand dollars from President Wilson's contingency fund for such a purpose—provided the people of Arkansas would contribute a similar amount. Brough appointed a special commission, chaired by A. B. Poe, to organize the fund-raising campaign. With Mrs. Brough and a number of prominent Little Rock citizens participating, the matching money was raised, and the legislature, as the governor requested, passed a measure adding the woman's reformatory to the state's correctional program.[29]

In the area of education, the 1919 legislature enacted a measure providing for county boards of education and for county superintendents, and another one by which Arkansas continued to accept the benefits of the federal law for the promotion of vocational training in agriculture, home economics, trades, and industries.[30]

Although Brough was a prolific letter writer, his letters dealing with personal and family matters constitute a relatively small portion of his papers. However, a number of letters in 1919 shed light on aspects of his life apart from politics, administration, and oratory. Early in January he wrote to his stepmother, Cora S. Brough (in Los Angeles), thanking her for the Christmas gift she sent, and relating sundry family news: Anne was enjoying their new home . . . her brother Granville and his wife were visiting the Broughs . . . Hillman's Aunt Mary was planning to visit soon . . . nephew Charlie (Knight and Fanny's son) was doing well in school . . . Hillman was in good health generally, but would probably have to have a hernia operation. Letters to Anne's parents, the Roarks, in Franklin, Kentucky, and to Knight in Vicksburg, reveal that a number of family members suffered ill health from time to time; Anne had a bout with influenza, Judge Roark suffered an unspecified illness, as did the governor's brother, Knight; and the governor himself occasionally referred to his hernia and the probability of an operation in August. Because of the anticipated hospitalization Brough declined to attend two meetings scheduled in August: a Brough family reunion at Gettysburg, Pennsylvania, and the governors' conference at Salt Lake City.[31]

Beginning in 1919 the governor undertook to acquire histories of all the states. He usually asked incumbent governors to procure these books for him, although, in the case of California, he asked his stepmother in Los Angeles to send him a history of that state. His letter to her stated his motivation for acquiring the collection: it was for his use in connection with a new position he would assume upon the conclusion of his term as governor in January 1921—chief publicity agent for a group of Arkansas businessmen who formed the nucleus of a state chamber of commerce. In September a Little Rock businessman named Roy Thompson, acting for himself and fifteen other individuals and firms, contracted with Brough to serve as publicity agent for four years, beginning with the expiration of his tenure as governor. Brough was to receive an annual salary of six thousand dollars, plus an annual expense account of four thousand. In addition, he would be permitted to earn additional income through chautauqua/lyceum lectures, but must remit half of such earnings to his employers. Each of the individuals and firms composing this incipient state chamber of commerce agreed to contribute three thousand dollars to carry out the contract with Brough.[32]

There are indications that during much of the year Brough had more than a passing interest in running for the Senate in 1920. He received considerable encouragement from various friends, and as late as July 2 asked one of them to write letters to relatives, requesting their support. However, by early October he had accepted the publicity job. Nor was he swayed by the prospect of re-entering the university environment; he turned down offers to become president of colleges in Mississippi and Oklahoma.[33]

Brough's activities in the summer of 1919 (in addition to making a number of speeches both within and outside the state) included calling a second special session of the Forty-Second General Assembly. Purposes of this special session were to amend certain road legislation enacted earlier in the year and to pass a law prohibiting profiteering and the hoarding of foodstuffs. The session convened in late September and passed numerous bills pertaining to road improvement, but decisively defeated the antiprofiteering measure which Brough strongly favored. A much-anticipated highlight of the session never occurred: an address by President Wilson, whose speechmaking itinerary included Little Rock on September 27. The president's sudden physical collapse on September 26 resulted in the cancellation of all his remaining speaking engagements.[34]

Soon after the September special legislative session adjourned, Arkansas's worst race riot in the twentieth century erupted in Phillips County. The governor, with authorization from Secretary of War Newton Baker, sent five hundred federal troops from Camp Pike to restore order. Before this was accomplished, at least five whites and twenty-five blacks had been killed. Brough accompanied the troops, and at one point some shots were fired just over the heads of the governor and his party, who were in an automobile. (Afterward, an old friend of the governor wrote him as follows: "I congratulate you on missing the bullet that was aimed at your venerable bald head.") Brough appointed a committee of Phillips County citizens to investigate the causes of the riots. The committee did so, and reached the conclusion that members of the Progessive Farmers and Household Union had organized the black sharecroppers for the purpose of carrying out a massacre of many of the white men in the area. This became the "official" cause of the rioting; Brough's private secretary, in a letter to one of Brough's friends in Texas, stated that if the governor had not acted as he did, ". . . the negroes would have wiped out three or four of those little towns down there in the Southern end of Phillips County." Brough himself accepted the "conspiracy theory" of the origins of the Elaine trouble, and felt that if federal troops had not been sent many more lives—both whites and blacks—would have been lost.[35]

This "official" interpretation was soon challenged by persons who found that the racial strife in Phillips County stemmed from the peonage to which most of the black tenant farmers and sharecroppers were subjected. One investigator, Walter White of the National Association for the Advancement of Colored People (NAACP), published his conclusions in several newspapers and in *The Nation*. White pointed out that individual sharecroppers, powerless to secure fair treatment from the plantation owners, turned to collective action by forming the Progressive Farmers and Household Union. Through this organization they hoped to go to court and get relief from peonage conditions. The first shots of the riot were fired near a rural black church where a branch of the union was holding a meeting. White and other critics of the "planned insurrection" theory also maintained that the Committee of Seven, in their investigation, coerced confessions from "suspects"; and that the seventy-three blacks who were indicted did not get a fair trial.[36]

Governor Brough's ready acceptance of the local white leaders' assessment of the racial conflict was consistent with his white supremacist views. While the tales of blacks planning to murder white citizens may appear far-fetched, it must be remembered that in the postwar months racial and labor strife, and rumors of communist and anarchist machinations, created an atmosphere of hysteria. During the war Brough, in patriotic speeches, had expressed concern over subversive activities of Bolsheviks and others opposed to the war effort. Thus he was disposed to go along with the views of the all-white Committee of Seven and to place blame on "outside agitators." Nonetheless, one might expect a more empirical attitude from a former professor who had chaired the University Commission on Race Questions. That commission, established by the Southern Sociological Congress, had studied the economic and social conditions of southern blacks and had made recommendations for their amelioration. It is ironic to note that among those who had applauded the commission's work, and Brough's role in it, was Scipio A. Jones, a black lawyer who was enlisted by the NAACP in its efforts on behalf of the convicted blacks of Elaine. In 1916 Jones had regarded Brough as a man who, as governor, would be supportive of the struggles of Arkansas blacks.[37]

Of sixty-five blacks indicted and tried, twelve were found guilty of first-degree murder and sentenced to die, but the NAACP provided counsel for the condemned men, and after years of complex litigation they were released.[38]

In the aftermath of the Elaine riots Brough appointed an inter-racial commission, being the first governor to do so. The commission, composed of nine whites and eight blacks, was to hold discussions regarding race problems, not only to foster more amicable relations, but to explore ways in which to secure equal justice for blacks and to improve their conditions with respect to housing, sanitation, and recreation. These efforts reflect the attitude of Brough and other progressive, paternalistic southerners: holding to their belief in white supremacy, but hoping and striving for amelioration and uplift beneficial to both races. However, critical references to the Elaine riots in newspapers and magazines continued to aggravate the state's image problem, even after Brough left office.[39]

During the last year of his tenure as governor, Brough, in addition to carrying out his administrative responsibilities, continued to be available for numerous speeches—for a variety of groups in a variety of places. However, in the summer and fall of 1920, he applied much of his energy and oratory to the Democratic party cause. Accompanied by his wife, he traveled to San Francisco as delegate-at-large for Arkansas, to the party convention. A scrapbook clipping from an unnamed newspaper reports that during the convention, William Jennings Bryan, at one point, seriously advanced Brough's name as a presidential possibility, and that delegates from about nine states seriously considered the Arkansas governor for the vice-presidential nomination. On the return trip the Broughs were honored guests at a banquet at Ogden, sponsored by the Ogden Chamber of Commerce. This was probably the highlight of the year for the governor, for it was a kind of homecoming: the toastmaster had been a friend of the governor during their youth; and numerous other acquaintances from those early years were renewed. The mayor of Ogden even recalled young Brough's speeches on behalf of Bryan and "free silver" in the nineties. Brough was the featured speaker at the dinner, and the Ogden press reported that he gave an eloquent address.[40]

As he had done in 1912 and 1916, Brough campaigned devotedly for the 1920 Democratic cause, delivering speeches for the James Cox-Franklin Roosevelt ticket in Missouri, Iowa, Illinois, Ohio, West Virginia, New York, and Maine. He seems to have been well received; for example, an Ohio newspaper commented that Brough had a pleasing personality and was knowledgeable about "almost any topic," and a Parkersburg, West Virginia, paper described his speech as the finest heard in that city in years. The *Arkansas Democrat* observed that the state of Arkansas was greatly honored by having Governor Brough and Sen. Joseph T. Robinson—who had been named chairman of the San Francisco convention—play such significant roles on behalf of the Democratic party:

> Never before, perhaps, has Arkansas been accorded the national recognition it has obtained through the ability of [these two] representatives.[41]

The efforts of Brough and other campaign orators failed to avert the landslide victory by Warren G. Harding in the November election. Nonetheless, newspaper coverage of Brough's campaign speeches clearly show that he made a favorable impression on large numbers of the party faithful in many states. Meanwhile, he was not uninvolved in Democratic politics in Arkansas. For a time he supported Smead Powell for the Democratic gubernatorial nomination, and in so doing drew severe criticism from a rival contender, Thomas C. McRae. Prior to the August primary, Brough announced that he was switching allegiance due to Powell's "low road" campaign tactics; he now supported McRae, who won the nomination. Despite Brough's switch, McRae remained quite critical of some of the governor's policies and was a determined opponent of the Arkansas Corporation Commission, whose creation Brough regarded as one of his administration's greatest accomplishments. Some Arkansans criticized the governor as being too lenient in granting pardons to prisoners, and others expressed discontent with the road improvement program, the heavy cost of which would rest on property owners in the respective improvement districts. Controversy over the road program would be spotlighted in the *New York Times* within months after the governor left office.[42]

Such negative reactions to Brough's leadership may explain why some contemporary observers did not believe he could have won the Senate race in 1920. However, evidences of the governor's continued popularity are abundant. In 1920 he was held in high esteem by many citizens who applauded his stand on prohibition, his war-time leadership, his progressive policies, and his contributions to an upgrading of the state's image. Brough himself took pride in the progressive accomplishments of his administration, and in a statement made near its close discussed those achievements which were a "source of gratification" to him: (1) strengthening the state's educational system; (2) improvement of the physical well-being of the state's prisoners; (3) reform of the tax assessment process; (4) taking a strong stand in favor of woman suffrage; (5) creation of the Boys' Industrial School, the Girls' Industrial School, and the Women's Reformatory; (6) advertising the state of Arkansas, sparing "neither my health nor my personal comfort" in this task; and (7) placing the state on a cash basis, which Brough regarded as "unquestionably the greatest achievement of my administration." To these could be added a number of other progressive achievements; indeed, if Brough is to be evaluated according to the goals he set and his success in accomplishing them, one must conclude that he was highly effective as governor.[43]

The governor's decision to retire from politics (at least for a time) was made several months before the primary race of 1920. He apparently believed he could have been elected to the Senate, but maintained that he could serve Arkansas better in a public relations role than in a Republican-controlled Senate. The anticipated high cost of the campaign was also a deterrent; besides, he was promised an attractive income from both the state chamber of commerce and the Redpath-Vawter chautauqua organization.[44]

Perhaps the governor also looked forward to at least temporary relief from the strains and stresses of political office. The speechmaking role that awaited him when he left office was expected to be strenuous—but far less so than dealing with legislatures and intraparty squabbles. Upon his retirement he received numerous tributes from the press, various politicians, and numerous citizens, many of whom fully expected him to return eventually to the political arena.[45]

The Roark home in
Franklin, Kentucky.
Courtesy of Price Roark.

Charles Hillman Brough as a
student at Mississippi College, 1894.
Courtesy of Price Roark.

Hillman College, Clinton, Mississippi. *Courtesy of Price Roark.*

Anne Roark Brough. *Courtesy of Price Roark.*

Anne Roark. *Courtesy of Price Roark.*

Charles Hillman Brough as
a professor at Mississippi
College, around 1900.
Courtesy of Price Roark.

Charles Milton Brough at
his Los Angeles home,
1908. With him are his son
Knight and grandson
Charlie, age three.
Courtesy of Price Roark.

This photograph of Brough
was used in a promotional
brochure for lyceum lectures.
Courtesy of Price Roark.

The Brough home in
Fayetteville. *Courtesy of
Price Roark.*

The Brough residence at 1404
Scott Street in Little Rock.
Courtesy of Price Roark.

Young Charles Milton Brough,
the governor's nephew.
Courtesy of Price Roark.

Young Charles Hillman
Brough. *Courtesy of
Price Roark.*

Flora Thompson Brough. *Courtesy of Price Roark.*

Charles Milton Brough.
Courtesy of Price Roark.

Governor Brough, *center, with scroll,* at a patriotic rally in Little Rock during World War I. *Special Collections, Mullins Library, University of Arkansas, Fayetteville.*

Ogden, Utah, in the 1880s. *John P. Soule Collection, Special Collections, University of Utah Library, Salt Lake City.*

Nelson Hall, Mississippi College at Clinton. *Mississippi Department of Archives and History, Jackson, Mississippi.*

This photograph of Brough was probably made following his graduation from Johns Hopkins in 1898. *Arkansas History Commission, Little Rock.*

Governor Brough, *front row, center, in light-colored suit and bow tie,* woman suffragists, and others, following passage in 1917 of a bill granting women the right to vote in primary elections. *Arkansas History Commission, Little Rock.*

Washington Boulevard, Ogden, Utah, around the 1890s. *Utah State Historical Society, Salt Lake City, Utah.*

Bruce Hall, Central Baptist College, Conway, Arkansas. *Recent photograph by the author.*

CHAPTER 5

Chautauqua Headliner, 1921–25

D R. BROUGH TOOK DELIGHT in educating people, whether as a college professor, a Sunday School teacher, or as an orator. During his years in academe he delivered speeches on a wide variety of occasions, and a few of his speaking engagements were for local chautauqua programs. He believed that the chautauqua—along with the lyceum—was an effective channel both for disseminating information and for upholding traditional American values, and following his terms as governor he turned much of his energy and talent in this direction. He became a "headliner" for one of the largest of the traveling chautauqua organizations, while at the same time fulfilling his contract with Arkansas business leaders to advertise and promote Arkansas. From 1921 to 1925 Brough logged many miles and delivered many patriotic and uplifting speeches; but the beginning and close of this period in his life were marked by serious health problems.

On the day following his retirement from the governor's office, Brough entered St. Luke's Hospital in Little Rock to have a hernia operation, surgery which was needed for several months, but postponed. Doctors had advised him at least to take some rest, but instead the governor had maintained a strenuous work schedule during his last months in office, including a hard speaking campaign in the fall of 1920, traveling in a number of states on behalf of the national Democratic ticket. Soon after his operation it appeared that he was recuperating, and in response to that news the Arkansas Senate, by unanimous vote, adopted a resolution of gratification on the ex-governor's recovery. However, he experienced several relapses over the next three and a half months and did not return to his normal vigor until mid-summer.[1]

Brough's first relapse, the first week in February, kept him in the hospital several more weeks, but by early March he was back at home on Scott Street.

In late March (21 or 22) he suffered a much more severe setback; an infected bladder, nephritis, and cardiac irregularities were among the complications contributing to what doctors described as a grave condition. Anne, Knight, doctors, and friends kept vigil at his bedside, and newspaper reports indicated that Brough was near death. A Vicksburg editor offered an almost eulogistic commentary on the former governor: "He was the same affable, courteous, generous-hearted man as governor of a state, as he was before he ever aspired to . . . being governor of Arkansas." A front-page headline in the *Fort Smith Southwest American* was gloomy indeed, stating that Brough was dying.[2]

During these critical weeks there were scores of telephone calls (many long distance), letters, and telegrams inquiring about Brough's condition and expressing hopes and prayers for his recovery. Many of the well-wishers were from New England and the Middle West, where the governor had recently delivered political speeches for the Democratic national ticket. One letter, handwritten, was from William Jennings Bryan, writing from his winter home in Miami. As Brough began to rally in early April, with more normal pulse and respiration, his physician, Dr. O. A. Carruth, issued a statement concerning his patient's relapse. Brough, the doctor said, had been an unusually active and energetic governor who, in tackling the strenuous and exacting duties of office, had thrown his whole strength into the effort and never spared himself. Responding to every call, he used up his vitality and retained no reserve strength to bolster him in his present illness.[3]

Throughout April Brough made slow but steady progress—but suffered another relapse on May 11 and returned to the hospital, where he immediately underwent three blood transfusions (his brother, Knight, was one of the donors). Rapid recovery followed; he returned home on May 25, and in early June was resting and recuperating at Knight's home in Vicksburg. During this convalescence visit he gave several addresses, beginning with a speech before the local Kiwanis Club. By early July the *Vicksburg Daily Herald* observed that Brough would soon be ready to assume his work with the businessmen's group which comprised a kind of state chamber of commerce and to begin his chautauqua obligations for 1921. Brough and his wife planned to visit friends in Jackson (including the governor and his wife), then travel to Nashville where they would visit friends and relatives. From Nashville they would travel to Franklin, Kentucky, and spend some time with Anne's parents. In the interview for the Vicksburg article the former governor appeared to be "on the job" of boosting Arkansas, as he had done so many times as governor; he discussed Arkansas's resources—bauxite, coal, lead, zinc, manganese, diamonds, timber, and all kinds of food products. As for roads,

Brough spoke of recent progress in adding more miles of paved highways—such as the Little Rock-Eudora connection. The article noted that Brough, as head of the state chamber of commerce, aimed to mobilize every resource to put new life in old industries as well as develop new ones.[4]

After about six weeks in Vicksburg Brough, weighing 153 pounds, appeared to be fully restored to his old-time vitality and energy. He and Anne spent an enjoyable and restful month with her parents in Franklin. Writing to a banker friend, Brough said, "[W]e have good games of rook, go auto-riding, sleep late, and eat everything in sight." He described the days as "fearfully hot," but said the nights were cool. The man he was writing, Virgil C. Pettie of England, had written to Mrs. Brough as well as her husband, expressing concern about Brough's eagerness to begin his chautauqua lectures and his long-delayed work for the state chamber of commerce. Pettie hoped he would wait until fall, rather than risk a setback in health; but since Brough was determined to get back to work August 1, Pettie was glad Mrs. Brough was to accompany him on his lecture circuit, so she could watch over him.[5]

The ex-governor's anxiety to start his chautauqua lectures—and his duties for the state chamber of commerce—is understandable in view of his financial situation. Apparently he had no large accumulation of funds at the close of his tenure as governor; he had cited shortage of money as a reason for not making the Senate race in 1920. Indeed, it has been observed that Brough was probably the only governor who retired after four years in office poorer than when he was first inaugurated. The Broughs' purchase of their home on Arch Street, which was their residence after 1922, was made with money Anne inherited upon the death of her father, Judge Roark. (Anne's mother lived with them at the Arch Street home until her death in 1926.) Perhaps Brough's need to strengthen his financial situation explains his willingness to assume rigorous chautauqua and lyceum schedules, as well as his "sandwiching in" a variety of other speaking engagements for additional honoraria. (Although this might be a specious conclusion, in view of the "workhorse" character he had exhibited since his college days.)[6]

Brough's critical illness in the winter and spring of 1921 prevented him from drawing a salary from any source until about September 1. Writing to Virgil Pettie on July 15, he reflected his anxiety to return to work:

> my critical sickness of last winter and this spring has already cost me $3500, exclusive of the loss of a salary, under the contract, of $833.33 per month— meaning a total loss to me of nearly $8000. I feel that I must begin my Chautauqua work August first.[7]

Virgil C. Pettie was one of the principal founders of a recently formed organization of Arkansas boosters known as the Arkansas Advancement Association, whose purposes were "to advertise the natural resources of the State of Arkansas, and to advance the industrial, commercial and agricultural interests of its citizens." This association eventually took over Brough's contract with the "Chamber of Commerce" businessmen.[8]

Before beginning his summer chautauqua tour in 1921, Brough addressed the congregation of the Franklin Baptist Church on the topic, "The Christ of History." As usual, he received a highly favorable press report. Days later, on August 1, Brough launched out on a forty-three-speech tour for the Redpath Bureau. Accompanied by Anne, he followed a circuit in Missouri and Iowa for six weeks. His speech for most, if not all stops, was on "America's Leadership in the World."[9]

In this address he stressed America's commitment to service, which was based on her position of leadership among the Anglo-Saxon, Christian peoples. America also dominated the world in business, and in educational and literary accomplishments. America could become even greater by improving its roads, developing vocational education, and taking the lead in arms reduction efforts. As always, Brough received very favorable press coverage of his chautauqua performances; an Albany, Missouri, newspaper observed that it was understandable why Arkansas people "took this fine speaker and educator out of the State university and placed him in the Governor's chair." Despite the strenuous schedule of a daily lecture until September 12, plus occasional appearances as guest speaker for civic organizations, Brough gained strength and weight during the 1921 chautauqua season. Mrs. Brough accompanied him on most, if not all of this season's tour, but after 1921 she remained at their home in Little Rock, where she received and forwarded mail to her husband on the chautauqua circuit (or lyceum circuit, in winter months).[10]

At times during the 1921 chautauqua tour the Broughs were guests at special luncheons, such as the one by the Chamber of Commerce at Maryville, Missouri. On these occasions—as well as in the opening portions of his regular chautauqua (or lyceum) lectures—Brough would take a few moments to boost Arkansas. In his chautauqua presentations he would begin by complimenting the local community as well as the state, then bring the people greetings from Arkansas. This was usually followed by a brief refutation of Arkansas's negative image and glowing comments about his state's achievements and prospects. Sometimes he injected a bit of humor into his boosting; for example, he told a Fulton audience that Arkansans could claim to be a chosen people, since their state was the only one mentioned in the Bible: "Noah looked out of the Ark and saw . . ."[11]

Thus Brough's responsibilities to the chautauqua and lyceum circuits were interrelated with his "advertise Arkansas" role in the period 1921–25. However, since his role as defender and booster of Arkansas included a much longer period, and was so closely connected to the state's perennial image problem, that topic will be given special treatment in the following chapter; the remainder of the present chapter will focus on Brough as chautauqua and lyceum orator.

The original chautauqua assembly, founded in New York in the 1870s, inspired many imitators, as communities all over America organized independent summer programs which they labeled "chautauqua." A variety of talent was provided each summer—musicians, lecturers, artists, one-man dramatic presentations. Although independent chautauquas continued to be popular, the development which enabled summer chautauquas to have a really significant impact on American culture was the formation of talent bureaus which offered packaged programs to organized chains of towns. The bureaus and community leaders agreed on a contract which guaranteed the former a specified amount of money for providing several days' talent. After completing contracts with the communities and with the participants (lecturers, for example), a chautauqua agency would work out rather complex railroad connections in order to supply talent for all the communities in the "circuit." The lyceum movement, which actually antedated all varieties of chautauqua, was in a sense the winter counterpart of the summer programs. Lyceum programs were usually presented at night, in auditoriums, churches, and schoolhouses instead of tents; and the attractions were distributed over the entire season rather than scheduled for one week of nightly entertainment. Many of the talent bureaus—such as Redpath-Vawter—had divisions for both winter lyceums and summer chautauquas.[12]

For three decades the summer chautauquas brought culture to countless villages and towns throughout the nation. In addition to lecturers like William Jennings Bryan there were bands, orchestras, violinists, and play companies. Ministers announced the impending arrival of chautauqua; businessmen closed stores during the afternoon presentations; and farmers drove in from the country to attend sessions. In the weeks preceding the opening, local citizens boosted the program in nearby towns and worked diligently to sell advance tickets. The chautauqua movement reached its peak in popularity in the 1920s. In 1922, more than 35 million single-admission tickets were bought and used; and another 35 million lyceum tickets were purchased. Theodore Roosevelt once called chautauqua the "most American thing in America," and a writer in the 1920s agreed:

Scorn us if you will as we rattle home in the late evening with our Ford full of sleepy children: but nowhere else under the quiet stars at that moment will you find a more characteristic expression of the American Idea.[13]

In the early years of the circuit chautauquas many of the lecturers dealt with controversial issues—such as the graduated income tax, juvenile courts, pure food laws, and free textbooks. Advocates of these and other causes found the chautauqua platforms most useful in persuading large numbers of listeners that something must be done. By the mid-1920s, however, controversial topics had been largely supplanted by inspirational and patriotic themes, which students of the chautauqua and lyceum have labeled "Mother, Home, and Heaven." Although the various bureaus had earned a reputation for encouraging free discussion of issues, conservative community leaders sometimes intervened to prevent the appearance of a speaker whose ideas they considered hostile to their economic interests. For example, when Carl Thompson contracted with the Redpath organization in 1924 to deliver 103 lectures favoring public ownership of natural resources (water power, coal, oil, gas), certain business leaders in two cities succeeded in forcing the cancellation of his lecture. Also, a conservative newspaper editor in the territory denounced Thompson as "a socialist, a false prophet . . . and a companion of those who sought to overthrow the American government."[14]

Except for support of the League of Nations, which he sometimes stated in his "America's Leadership" speech, and criticism of the prohibition amendment on at least one occasion, Brough—like his friend (and hero), William Jennings Bryan—adhered to the inspirational and patriotic themes. This was true of his early association with summer chautauquas as well as his more expanded activities in the 1920s. One of his earliest chautauqua speeches, "Our Union and Our State," was delivered at an independent chautauqua while Brough was a professor at Mississippi College. No doubt this oration was calculated to stir pride in both Mississippi and America, while another lecture he developed soon after, on "The Glory of the Old South and the Greatness of the New," was aimed at regional and national pride. Brough continued to make summer chautauqua appearances after joining the University of Arkansas faculty, and in addition did some lyceum lecturing. Following his tenure as governor, this activity greatly increased; during four seasons, 1921–25, his "chautauqua trail" crossed thirty-eight states. (And sandwiched in between the circuit assignments were commencement addresses and addresses to fraternal, educational, and religious groups.) As noted previously, the speech he gave most frequently was "America's Leadership in the World"—which he had delivered more than three thousand times by 1932.[15]

Although it is doubtful that Dr. Brough would approve of "muzzling" a controversial speaker like Thompson, it is clear that he saw the role of the chautauqua and lyceum as that of upholding traditional values and conservative ideas. This is evident not only from the subject matter of his own lecture, but also from an article published in the *Arkansas Gazette* and a speech delivered at a banquet sponsored by his most frequent chautauqua employer, the Redpath Bureau. He believed that chautauqua and lyceum lecturers did an excellent job of satisfying the average citizen's "infinite hunger for information," but maintained that in doing so they should uphold the "old-fashioned conservatism and morality" of their audiences. Brough regarded chautauqua as "Main Street's Summer School," and pointed out that the average citizens who participated in it had little interest in "eccentric opinions," but were seeking "the main truths of life." He praised the Redpath organization for helping to provide a counter-weight to radicalism; the "tents of conservatism," he said, had rendered a great service in protecting the American people from "the wiles of Bolshevism, IWW-ism, and other forms of un-Americanism."[16]

During his busiest period on the circuits (1921–25) Brough continued to be well received by his audiences, and in one season enjoyed the highest rating of the lecturers for the Redpath Chautauqua. He also continued to get favorable press comments on both his oratorical ability and his personality; a South Carolina newspaper called him a gentleman of the Old South, a polished scholar, and "a personality that cannot be resisted." He was consistently praised for his style and enthusiasm and eloquence and was described as "electrifying" his audience. An admirer of his wrote him insisting that he was the best qualified to take up the work of the great Bryan, following the Commoner's death in 1925. Because of Brough's "scholarship, Christian character, optimism, political and church experience, oratorical ability, [and] qualities of leadership," the letter said, Brough was the Elisha or Paul upon whom the mantle should fall.[17]

By 1924 Brough's usual salary for chautauqua and lyceum engagements was $250 per week plus expenses—often stated as "250 and rails," since lecturers and other "talent" generally traveled by train. In negotiating with a talent bureau he stated his price and added, in an untypical boastful tone, that he had no difficulty in booking his time at that figure. In the heyday of his chautauqua/lyceum work, when he was also being paid for advertising Arkansas, Brough was able to earn about $8,000 a year, plus expenses.[18]

In 1924 the energetic lecturer/booster found time to take an active part in national Democratic politics, as a delegate to the nominating convention, and later as one of the orators for the party's speakers' bureau. Brough was a delegate-at-large from Arkansas, and in June he and Mrs. Brough were among the passengers on a special train to New York City, whose Madison Square Garden was the site of the convention. Brough delivered the nominating speech on behalf of Sen. Joe T. Robinson, Arkansas's "favorite son" for the presidential nomination. Brough hailed Robinson as

> a proven leader, who can unite all factions of our party, heal all party wounds; a twentieth century crusader for the immortal principles of Democracy and Americanism.[19]

A New York newspaper cartoonist, illustrating an article about various convention personalities, caricatured Brough as an egg in a cup, and labeled him as a "hard-boiled Robinson booster." Brough and other Arkansas delegates hoped Robinson would be chosen as a compromise between Al Smith and William G. McAdoo, but the convention instead picked John W. Davis of West Virginia. Although disappointed at Robinson's failure to win the nomination, Brough regarded Davis as a "splendid standard-bearer" and pledged to work for him in the election campaign. He did so, making a number of speeches on behalf of the ticket and the "thoroughly progressive" platform; for example, at Democratic rallies in Wisconsin, Illinois, and Oklahoma. However, Brough's strictly political speeches were somewhat limited in 1924 by his chautauqua and lyceum lecture obligations. Once again, as in 1920, the Democratic cause was a losing one, and the Republicans, led by President Coolidge, remained in the ascendancy.[20]

An example of the complicated and hectic pace followed by Brough (and other chautauqua "talent") is the following schedule of train connections on the Redpath circuit in 1924: August 15—leave Indianapolis, 12:30 A.M., arrive Bloomington, Ill., 5:42 A.M.; leave Bloomington, 7:15 A.M., arrive Jacksonville, Ill., 10:50 A.M.; leave Jacksonville, 5:45 P.M., arrive Hannibal, 8:50 P.M.; August 16—leave Hannibal, 11:48 A.M., arrive Cameron Junction, 5:15 P.M.; leave Cameron Junction 7:35 P.M., arrive Gallatin 8:08 P.M. The agency's letter to Brough explaining these connections urged him to "be sure to verify this schedule at each starting point."[21]

Most of Brough's chautauqua contracts were with the Redpath-Vawter Bureau, but he also obtained bookings from other organizations, especially for winter lyceum engagements. At various times he "sold time" to the Allen Lyceum and Festival Bureau, the United Lyceum Bureau, the Antrim Lyceum Bureau, the McDonald-Bryan Bureau, and the Affiliated Lyceum and Chautauqua Bureau. A bit of difficulty arose when he inadvertently allowed himself to be booked by two competing agencies—United and Allen—for the same lecture season, which was apparently contrary to a gentlemen's agreement among the various bureaus.[22]

In late 1924 Brough looked forward to a full summer schedule with the Redpath Chautauqua organization, although he arranged to cancel some of his lyceum obligations for the closing weeks of 1925, as he anticipated assuming, by that time, some new responsibilities in education or business. In February he declined an appointment as publicity director for Ouachita College, but a few weeks later accepted the position of educational secretary for both Ouachita and Central College at Conway. The new job involved giving lectures on behalf of the colleges; thus Brough took on more oratorical responsibilities, while continuing his "advertise Arkansas" campaign and preparing for a strenuous chautauqua schedule. However, another health crisis—not as life-threatening, but more prolonged than the one in 1921—forced the cancellation of most of these obligations.[23]

On the advice of his doctors, Brough in the spring of 1925 had all of his teeth extracted—with disastrous results. Apparently suffering from an extreme reaction to the anesthesia, he entered upon a period of illness which culminated in a complete nervous breakdown and required months for recovery. As in 1921, Brough, accompanied by his wife, spent part of his recuperative period with Knight and his wife at Vicksburg, where the ailing ex-governor rested and waited for his dentures to be completed. Regretfully, he had to interrupt his newly begun work with the Baptist colleges, but their officials reacted with sympathy and understanding, and urged him not to worry about the delay. The president of Ouachita suggested that if Brough chose to forego his rigorous chautauqua lectures for the summer, he might find that to be an appropriate time to resume the less demanding work of educational secretary.[24]

Despite his eagerness to resume all of his duties, Brough was unable to repeat the relatively rapid recovery of 1921. The middle of May found him still in Vicksburg, suffering from unsettled nerves. Although his false teeth were difficult to get used to, he believed that he could articulate well enough to deliver speeches without them. It was lack of strength to maintain the high standards of Redpath Chautauqua that worried him. For a time it appeared that he would be sufficiently recovered to undertake the summer circuit at its beginning in early June. Anticipating that, he wrote to an official of the bureau regarding its plans to "motorize" the schedule—which meant using cars rather than the train to transport talent from point to point. Brough, whose doctors had forbidden him to drive, requested arrangements be made for him to continue traveling by rail. In reply the official indicated that cars would be the mode of transportation, but that the governor would have a driver. He also expressed hope that no substitutions for Brough would have to be found and that he would be able to fulfill the entire speaking schedule. However, it was mid-July before Brough, Anne, and the doctors deemed the patient ready to begin lecturing again.[25]

Having canceled over a month of his summer engagements with Redpath, Brough wrote the Redpath Chautauqua manager on July 15 that he was "ready for the fray" and hoped to render good service, beginning with his Greenfield, Ohio, appearance. But after filling only two lecture engagements —Greenfield and Columbus—he was physically exhausted and found it necessary to cancel the remainder of his contract. More than a year later, after periods of rest and convalescence in Ludington, Michigan, Milwaukee, and Asheville, North Carolina, he acknowledged that he had suffered a "complete nervous breakdown." Late in 1925, when he believed he had recovered sufficiently to assume a scaled-down work schedule, he accepted the position of director of the Arkansas Public Service Information Bureau (APSIB), a type of chamber of commerce organized by a number of public utility companies. He managed to do some work for the APSIB during or between rest periods in 1925–26; for example, he published a newsletter in which he predicted excellent economic growth for Arkansas in 1926 and stressed the importance of keeping up the advertising of the state's resources and promise for industrial development. Apparently the new organization was not very different in purpose from the Advancement Association, which Brough continued to serve as vice-president. Whether he retained the position with Ouachita and Central Colleges is difficult to determine. However, it is clear that Brough's health setback effectively terminated the hectic, grueling summer chautauqua schedules, although after his recovery he continued to engage in extensive public speaking on politics, education, religion, et cetera, and occasionally lectured for an independent chautauqua. Brough's retirement from the rigorous circuit schedules coincided, more or less, with the general decline of chautauqua and the lyceum. Actually, a decline in the number of communities sponsoring chautauquas had begun around 1922, and by 1930 there were fewer than 10 percent as many towns with annual chautauquas as in 1921. Of these, about 75 percent had populations of fewer than fifteen hundred. Nineteen twenty-five—the year of Brough's exit—was a disappointing year, even to the larger bureaus like Redpath-Vawter. Keith Vawter, director of the firm, was alert to the trends; he sold his talent contracts to other bureaus, and he sold all of his tents. The heyday of "culture under canvas" was over, and the future signified to men like Vawter the further decline of this means of bringing information and entertainment to Main Street America. Modern forces like radio, the automobile, and the cinema offered alternative cultural opportunities which were formidable competitors.[26]

After leaving the chautauqua and lyceum circuits, and following an extensive period, Brough recovered sufficiently to assume responsibilities in higher education. Before examining these developments, however, his work as Arkansas's pre-eminent "booster"—both before and after 1925—deserves special consideration.

CHAPTER 6

Talking Arkansas Up, 1921–31

*A*S WE HAVE SEEN, Governor Brough, more than a year before the end of his second term, had signed a contract with a group of Arkansas businessmen to serve as their publicity agent. The introductory paragraph of the contract noted that these business leaders, who regarded themselves as a kind of state chamber of commerce, "deemed it advisable to secure the services of some person of outstanding ability and reputation" to act as their publicity agent. Apparently they did not consider anyone for this role except the governor, who was almost certainly the best-qualified person for the job.[1]

Brough's credentials as Arkansas's chief advertiser included a thoroughly optimistic outlook on life, shaped in part, perhaps, by the Christian influences in Clinton and the "boom town" atmosphere of Ogden. Moreover, as he reached adulthood near the end of the century he seems to have imbibed the heady optimism of both the "New South" idea and the spread-eagle nationalism of the "New Manifest Destiny" ideology. These seemingly contradictory creeds were the source of two of his most popular speeches: "The Glory of the Old South and the Greatness of the New," and "America's Leadership of the World" (sometimes titled "The Americanization of the World"). In the first speech Brough, like other "New South" orators, extolled the "old ways" while asserting the dawn of regional economic and cultural progress. He depicted the chivalry, the valor, and the greatness of southern men and the loyalty and dignity of southern women. One press comment on the "South" lecture stated that the "audience listened with breathless silence as eloquence flowed like magic from the speaker's lips." Their regional pride was bolstered, while at the same time they were reassured that life was getting better! In addition to his praise for the Southland in general, Brough frequently delivered speeches for memorial groups organized for honoring specific Old South heroes, such as Robert E. Lee, Raphael Semmes, and Lucius Q. C. Lamar. His eulogizing reinforced the listeners' pride in these heroic figures from the past and perhaps left them feeling somewhat "unreconstructed." However, Brough did not intend to revive sectionalism as indicated in one of his recurring metaphors:

> I thank God that the last tear shed over the bier of the dying Confederacy has crystallized into a signet gem, betrothing the love of the new south to the brotherhood of American states . . .[2]

Much of Brough's writing, as well as his oratory, was characterized by what later generations would call an "up-beat" vein. One of his articles, "Loyalty to Mississippi" (*Mississippi College Magazine,* 1900) contains a considerable amount of economic history, but also includes extravagant praise of Mississippi and its leaders—such as Edward Walthall wielding a "spear . . . studded with the immortal truths of Southern statescraft." Another article in the college magazine, entitled "We Study but to Serve" (1901), was an exuberantly optimistic appeal to young Christians, and was filled with encouraging and inspirational passages:

> Christ has given us a religion of beauty and optimism.

> How beautiful is the world in which we live and move and have our being!

> [In America, as contrasted with non-Christian nations] . . . every man enjoys the priceless boon of life, liberty and the pursuit of happiness, redeemed, regenerated, and disenthralled as he is by the irresistible genius of universal emancipation.

Although he recognized that Christianity was "conceived in travail and in sorrow," and Christians, like Christ himself, must undergo suffering and hardships, Brough asserted a "social gospel" approach to religion, and maintained that the "refinement and charity of Christian life, the beauty of its ideas and intensity of its moral passions" led to the improvement of society as well as of individuals.[3]

We may assume that Brough's numerous commencement addresses were optimistic and full of promise for the graduating classes. And his summer speechmaking on behalf of Mississippi College (and later, the University of Arkansas) were further evidences of his skill as a promoter (or "booster"). His addresses to fellow educators also reflected his faith in the classroom teachers' ability to help children grow morally as well as intellectually. He told a group of Arkansas teachers that their influence over their pupils should inculcate in them, among other attitudes, a cheerful and optimistic outlook. As he surveyed the educational scene in Arkansas in the early 1900s, however, Brough's optimism was dampened by the state's deficiency in support for the schools. He remained confident, however, that Arkansas was "on the move" in this area as well as in economic and social progress, and as governor he placed educational advancement high on his agenda for progressive reforms.[4]

Brough's move to Arkansas in 1903 coincided with the publication of Thomas Jackson's *On a Slow Train through Arkansaw,* a joke book which became a bestseller and which did much to reinforce the already widespread perception of the state's inhabitants as backwoods hillbillies. Actually, the book did not concentrate on Arkansas; however, the title, and the Arkansas setting for the opening pages, tended to establish in the popular mind a special association with Arkansas. Since the book was sold at railroad newsstands, and since Brough was a frequent railroad traveler, one may assume that he was familiar with it some years before he was elected governor. In any case, it is apparent from numerous speeches he made as governor that he regarded Jackson as one of several "culprits" responsible for Arkansas's backward image. Addressing an organization of St. Louis businessmen he noted that Arkansas was making great strides along economic, educational, and moral lines, and no longer provided a theme for the "miserable diatribes" of Jackson and other wits. In this speech and others, Brough also censured the humorous philosopher and novelist Opie Read for helping perpetuate the backwards Arkansas idea. Brough was perhaps thinking about Read's role in disseminating the 'coonskin cap image of the "Arkansas Traveller" tale, as well as the frontier humor of Read's novels. (In time, some Arkansans acquired the mistaken notion that Read, rather than Jackson, had written the *Slow Train* volume; in 1944 a student of Read's work published an essay to correct this error.)[5]

Apart from the content of his promotional speeches, Brough's personality and oratorical eloquence were an excellent advertisement for Arkansas. A St. Louis editor made this observation:

> Time was when Arkansas could not send her chief executive outside the limits of the state without inviting ridicule. In Charles H. Brough she has a governor who is not only a splendid representative of her best citizenship, but who can hold his own in the company of able men. As an Arkansas exhibit he ranks right up there with the big red apples, delicious strawberries and other first class products of which the state is justly proud.

And the *Albany* (New York) *Times-Union* called Brough "a man of learning, eloquence, and adaptability and thoroughly versed in the practical affairs of life."[6]

In many of the governor's speeches the praise of Arkansas was confined
to a fairly brief introduction to a totally different topic—banking, politics,
patriotism, et cetera; and as noted in the previous chapter, this format characterized his chautauqua and lyceum presentations. On occasion, however,
Brough's paean to Arkansas's resources and potential was extensive; he seemed
determined to overwhelm his listeners with factual data. An example of this
approach is an address to the Missouri Bar Association in 1918, in which the
governor's catalog of positive things about Arkansas included apples and
peaches; cotton, corn, and rice acreage; mineral resources such as coal, lead,
zinc, slate; an abundance of ash, cottonwood, red gum, hickory, and oak; and
the only diamond mine in the Western Hemisphere. Brough claimed that
Arkansas's economic resources were limitless and that the state could exist
independently of the outside world. With regard to the latter claim, Brough
frequently stated that if a "Chinese Tatary Wall" were built around Arkansas,
its people could survive very well on their abundant resources. Whether or
not Brough originated this claim, it gained wide acceptance, and perhaps suggested a somewhat provincial attitude—thus, ironically, adding credence to
the image of an isolated, "outback" area.[7]

The widely traveled, highly educated professor/politician was no provincial, though, and he had no intention of fostering a provincial outlook among
his fellow Arkansans. In advertising Arkansas's resources he wanted to
encourage commercial and cultural contacts with other states; especially did
he wish to persuade northern businessmen to consider Arkansas for invest-
ment and expansion. He also worked at this goal by pressing for better roads,
which he believed would benefit business as well as agriculture. Brough managed to stay well informed about political and economic developments
throughout the nation, and in urging the legislature to pass progressive legislation habitually pointed to the examples of other states in enacting such
measures.[8]

The progressive reforms of his administration gave Brough additional items
for his catalog of Arkansas achievements—thus women's suffrage, educational
reforms, and good roads were given a place in his "booster" speeches, along
with the "brag talk" about timber, field crops, fruits, and mineral resources.

The booster spirit in Arkansas seemed to increase following the war (a
trend evident in many parts of the nation), owing largely to the governor's
efforts, but stemming also from the focus on 1919 as the centennial of the creation of Arkansas Territory. The *Arkansas Gazette* published a special supple-

ment whose illustrated cover contained assorted information, which could have been excerpted from a typical "booster" speech by Brough:

> ... modern methods ... in raising pure bred livestock
> The third State in rice
> The fifth cotton producing state
> [leadership] in bauxite ... and [production of] coal, zinc, and manganese
> Annual lumber production more than two billion feet
> Good roads ... all over the state
> [Famous for] ... apples, peaches, and strawberries[9]

During and immediately following Brough's term as governor—when he and other Arkansas leaders were doing some of their most fervent boosting—the state was the target of some of the most virulent diatribes by northern writers. Henry Louis Mencken, in 1917 and 1921, attacked the South in general, as well as specific states such as Arkansas, deploring the region's cultural aridity. In "Sahara of the Bozart" (1917), Mencken called the South "the bunghole of the United States." In 1921 he elaborated on Dixie's shortcomings and hurled some special barbs at Arkansas, whose "miasmatic jungles" he described as "trackless and unexplored." Mencken's comments on Arkansas were hardly a devastating attack and amounted to only a few lines in a seven-page article. Nonetheless, sensitive Arkansas citizens—especially business leaders, politicians, and newspaper editors—were deeply offended and reacted angrily. Virgil C. Pettie, president of the Arkansas Advancement Association (AAA; Brough's employer, beginning in 1921), supported by the *Arkansas Democrat* and the Lions' Club, urged an Arkansas congressman in Washington to seek legislative action against Mencken. They hoped Congress might succeed in having him *deported,* but soon learned that the sage was a citizen—a native American, in fact—and thus was exempt from such action. Other southern states in Mencken's anti-South articles included Georgia, where "liberated lower orders of whites ... borrowed the worst commercial bumptiousness of the Yankee and superimposed it upon a culture that, at bottom, is little removed from barbarism." And even Virginia had "fallen to the bombastic trivialities of the camp-meeting and the Chautauqua." (Whether Brough ever read this elitist allusion to chautauqua programs is not known.)[10]

Additional adverse publicity for Arkansas appeared in March 1921—on page one of the *New York Times.* The headline for the first in a series of articles proclaimed, "Arkansas Totters under Road Taxes and Czar-like Rule." The *Times* story (and subsequent ones) discussed the abuses arising from hundreds of road improvement laws, most of them passed during Brough's second term, which established virtually autonomous road improvement districts throughout the state. In each district, a road commissioner was given arbitrary authority in taxing property owners to pay interest on road bonds. In many instances, the *Times* reported, taxes were confiscatory in nature and provoked angry reaction in the community; in one district outraged taxpayers forced the commissioner to resign at gunpoint. The articles also pointed to examples of gross waste and extravagance by local officials in charge of road building.[11]

Governor Brough had wanted a road-building plan featuring greater state supervision and control, but had apparently concluded that the decentralized approach might work; and he considered the road legislation of 1919 among the progressive accomplishments of his administration. Brough's successor, Thomas McRae, had been very critical of the road program during the 1920 gubernatorial race, and in responding to the articles in the *Times* acknowledged that the road improvement system was deplorable. "The whole thing," he said, "is a scandal and a shame and the odor of it reaches to heaven." However, the governor believed the *Times* stories had exaggerated the gravity of the situation.[12]

The irony of this bad publicity is apparent. How Arkansas boosters would have savored front-page coverage of the state's resources and promise! And how great an emphasis Brough and other publicists had placed on good roads as a key to progress for agriculture, industry, and schools! Because the *Times* series appeared at a time when Brough was in precarious health due to complications from his hernia operation, he may not have kept abreast of the stories as they appeared. However, by mid-summer he was aware of the "bad press," and this knowledge no doubt reinforced his resolve to "talk Arkansas up" in his long-deferred job as the state's principal promoter and advertiser. In a letter to his banker friend Virgil Pettie in July, he wrote:

> There is no State in the Union where advertising of the right kind would pay [better] than in the case of Arkansas, with her varied resources, immense amount of unoccupied land, delightful climate, and yet in need of capital.[13]

Pettie was the principal figure in the recently organized Arkansas Advancement Association, created, as noted in the previous chapter, to advertise Arkansas's resources and to promote its economic interests. Other leaders included Harvey Couch and Clio Harper. The goals of the association were essentially those of the chamber of commerce group that had employed Brough, but the new organization was aimed at generating much broader support throughout the state; its by-laws provided that the board of directors include one citizen from each county. In addition, the board would have eight at-large members and ten from Little Rock (in addition to the representative of Pulaski County). Pettie was enthusiastic about the association's potential for telling the "Arkansas story." Pettie was also enthusiastic about recruiting Brough to shoulder a large share of this promotional campaign. To do this the association would have to arrange with the "chamber" group to take over their contract with the ex-governor. Pettie, and apparently other association leaders, were eager to accomplish the transfer. Writing to Brough (who was in Franklin with Anne and her parents), Pettie reported on the sentiment he found at an association rally in Morrilton: "Everybody is enthused and all the people wanted Dr. Brough and wanted to take over his contract." One person at that gathering observed that Brough could do more to advertise Arkansas than all preceding governors had done. Pettie was confident that the assumption of Brough's contract—with the same salary, conditions, et cetera—could be effected by the middle of September, when Brough was scheduled to complete a chautauqua lecture tour. The contract take-over did occur, although evidence is lacking as to the exact date of the change. Brough was amenable to working for the association in the same role he had accepted from the chamber businessmen.[14]

One of the first publications of the association was a lengthy pamphlet entitled *Are You Interested in Arkansas?* The authors—Pettie, who was president of the association, and Clio Harper, the secretary—announced that the organization intended to spend one hundred thousand dollars annually in acquainting the world with Arkansas's resources and advantages. The money was to be raised through popular subscription in the various counties. No difficulty in raising the money was anticipated; citizens would surely see the need for the AAA campaign, in view of "recent unfavorable publicity." The reference was to the *New York Times* series on the Arkansas road situation, described above, and misleading accounts of the Elaine race riot. The pamphlet hinted that the *Times* front-page stories about Arkansas roads were motivated by a deliberate plan to besmirch the state's image. The authors noted that even the World War did not make page one of the *Times* with as much consistency as the stories on Arkansas road problems. As for the Elaine riot, the pamphlet charged that some who wrote about it continually misstated the facts. A "correct" telling of the story would show that the people of Phillips County were law abiding and that the Negroes there (and throughout Arkansas) were well-treated, ". . . and, for the most part, contented, progressive and prosperous."[15]

The challenge was for Arkansans to rally for an all-out effort to secure some positive publicity about their state. And this effort must begin by awakening Arkansas residents themselves to the good things about Arkansas:

If the majority of our citizens do not know how much better Arkansas is than the average state, how can we expect the residents of other states to give us credit for such remarkable resources? Until we take steps to enlighten them, we must expect the residents of other states to continue to hold Arkansas lightly.

The association pamphlet proceeded to outline a campaign of propaganda for use both within and outside the state. One device to be used was lapel buttons. The AAA planned to distribute buttons for Arkansas people traveling in other states. The buttons would read, "I Am Proud of Arkansas." Other buttons would be supplied to ticket agents of all railroad lines and to hotels within the state. These buttons would be given to travelers from other states, who would be encouraged to wear them; they read, "I Have Been to Arkansas and I Like It." Other "boost Arkansas" plans included (1) an "Arkansas Day" in New York City, featuring exhibits about the state, perhaps in the principal hotels; (2) a campaign to get favorable stories about Arkansas in numerous newspapers and magazines, including the "big" publications like *Saturday Evening Post* and *Literary Digest*; (3) a drive to acquaint the world with Arkansas products; for example, persuading advertisers of manufactured products to inform customers when the raw materials were of Arkansas origin; and (4) supplying Arkansas data to Arkansans on the lecture platform. (Brough, who was the foremost of the latter group, was always well armed with statistics and other information, but he apparently "dug" most of it out himself, without much dependence on "suppliers.")[16]

In July 1921, some days before he began his chautauqua lecture tour, Brough wrote a promotional article entitled "The New Arkansas." The article appeared in the January 1922 issue of the monthly periodical *Candid Opinion*, published at Prescott, Arkansas. The editor of this periodical was apparently quite concerned about the state's image problem; throughout the twenties he ran a number of articles on the subject, including a piece by Pettie in September 1921, setting forth the purposes of the Advancement Association. Brough's article was among his first efforts as "official" booster for Arkansas; at the time of composition he was still employed by the chamber of commerce group, although one paragraph pays tribute to Pettie and other leaders of the Advancement Association. Brough began the article as he frequently opened his speeches—with a brief refutation of Arkansas's negative image:

Arkansas, which was once cartooned as the land of the Arkansas Traveler, wearing his coon-skin cap and coming to the fork of the road, not knowing which fork to take, is entering upon a new era and is rapidly "building more stately mansions for its soul. . . ." Its twentieth century shibboleth is progress; its objectives are peace and prosperity and citizenship "redeemed, regenerated, and disenthralled by the irresistible genius of educational enlightenment."

Brough proceeded with comments about the state's "salubrious climate" and "life-giving waters"—language reminiscent of nineteenth-century promotional tracts—and remarked that Arkansas was truly "the Nation's Wonder State." (Some years later he claimed to have been the first to apply this label, which replaced "Bear State" as the state's nickname in 1923.) After a lengthy, statistics-filled salute to Arkansas agriculture, timber industry, and mineral resources, including oil, Brough alluded jokingly to the "slow train" theme, noting that Arkansas scenery was so entrancing that travelers *wanted* the trains to slow down![17]

Brough proceeded to extol Arkansas's recent educational progress—such as (1) increases in children enrolled in public schools, average daily attendance, teachers' salaries, per capita spending per pupil; (2) a decrease in the number of illiterate persons from 142,854 in 1910 to 121,837 in 1921; and (3) a variety of educational reforms, including the introduction of vocational training. Recognizing that much remained to be done, he urged Arkansas citizens to realize that the state's most important business was rising from its forty-sixth place in educational rank among the states.[18]

With regard to roads, he expressed pride in the progressive program begun during his administration and insisted that it would "ultimately be of untold benefit. . . ." Conceding that some mistakes had occurred, by virtue of the emphasis on local legislation, he decried the "scurrilous attacks" (referring mainly to the *New York Times* articles) upon the good name of Arkansas and cited an article in the *Outlook* which claimed that 98 percent of Arkansas citizens were fully satisfied with the road program.[19]

Brough also paid tribute to Arkansas's gifted writers, artists, and musicians and to its moral and religious strengths. Since it had such a small number of foreign-born citizens, Arkansas was a citadel of Americanism. Moreover, its church members, numbering more than 350,000, could be counted on to stand firm against Darwinism. Brough concluded with a stirring apostrophic passage, variations of which he used in many of his speeches:

Henceforth, Oh Arkansas, we look up to thee,
Not down at other states,
Arise, arise, be not proud, be humble and be wise
And bow thy head to the great Unknown One
Who on high, hath willed
that, as a state, Arkansas shall never die.[20]

Brough probably had a part in the Arkansas Advancement Association's lengthy "information sheet" which appeared in the *Congressional Record* in 1922. This catalog of "several hundred interesting facts" about "the nation's wonder state" was entered into the *Record* by Arkansas congressman Henderson M. Jacoway of Dardanelle. In a short preamble, Jacoway pointed out the approach of Arkansas's eighty-sixth anniversary of statehood. During those eighty-six years, he said, Arkansas had "wrought wondrously and well," and wished to publish her great achievements "to the world at large." He predicted that her future achievements would surpass those of the past, and she would become a ". . . national model worthy of . . . emulation by . . . her sister states."[21]

The first paragraph of the Advancement Association's information sheet on the Wonder State contained an answer to critics like Mencken who regarded Arkansas as remote and uncivilized: "Arkansas is not a wilderness, neither is it a frontier State. . . . There are no swamps nor large bodies of standing water. . . ." On the contrary, the state consists of law-abiding citizens who are ambitious for the welfare of their youth, as attested by its "excellent schools." Following these far-from-modest assertions is a veritable barrage of statistics, covering approximately four full pages of the *Record*. A list of sixty trees of commercial importance is followed by an "Alphabet of Arkansas Minerals," which gives at least one mineral for each letter of the alphabet. The remainder of the information sheet is a wide variety of statements about the state's economy, geographic characteristics, recreational opportunities, and livestock.[22]

Among the projects which Brough, Pettie, and others contrived for advertising Arkansas was the Arkansas Traveling Exposition Train (the "Booster Special"), which toured a number of eastern states in the fall of 1923 and 1924, carrying Arkansas citizens as well as displays of Arkansas agricultural, mineral, and manufactured products. This project was reminiscent of an earlier one in 1912; in that year an exposition train called "Arkansas on Wheels" had journeyed forth to advertise the state's resources and opportunities. Brough was among the notables traveling on the 1923 train, and addressed a crowd of well-wishers at the railroad depot prior to the special train's departure from Little Rock. The 1923 train visited Washington, D.C., New York City, Boston, Buffalo, Cleveland, and Indianapolis. Brough and other passengers judged the exposition trains as highly effective in advertising the state's resources; an estimated one hundred thousand persons visited the train and viewed its exhibits at the various cities. The minerals displayed on the 1924 Booster Special were sufficiently impressive to receive mention in a newsletter published by the

American Mining Congress. Although Brough's lyceum lecture schedule in 1924 did not permit him to travel with the exposition train, he did join the company of Arkansas travelers at one or two of their stops in the northeast.[23]

While advertising the greatness of Arkansas, Brough and other boosters were, of course, aware of certain deficiencies—such as low ranking in education (despite noteworthy progress) and the decline in cotton prices after 1920. But they were confident of overcoming these problems and were convinced that a necessary step in doing so was the erasure of the negative image which had beset the state for so long. Brough and others involved in the Advancement Association's efforts began calling Arkansas the "Wonder State," which soon supplanted the old nickname, "the Bear State." The old name was thought to perpetuate the backwoodsy, "coonskin cap" image. Many state lawmakers also preferred "Wonder State," and in 1923 the general assembly passed a resolution formally adopting the new nomenclature. The resolution contained typical "brag talk," such as the assertion that it was "an admitted fact" that Arkansas's resources surpassed those of any other state.[24]

In due time—around 1931—H. L. Mencken would engage in further "Arkansas bashing," but in the meantime that role was assumed by C. L. Edson, in an article in *Nation* entitled "Arkansas: A Native Proletariat." This article, which contained some of the most scathing diatribes ever published about Arkansas, was published in the May 1923 issue—ironically, soon after the proud claims issuing from the Congress and the state legislature. Edson's piece was number 28 in a series the magazine was running on "These United States." Edson attacked not only contemporary Arkansans but their forebears as well; he said the state's people were descended from "three generations of American roughneck blood with no trace of gentility." The inhabitants had no ambition: their unofficial motto was, "I've never seen nothin', I don't know nothin', I hain't got nothin', and I don't want nothin'." Calling Arkansas a land of illiteracy, Edson claimed that few of the people could read, and those who could chose not to, preferring their own legends, jokes, and fables. A scornful attitude toward "history and letters and . . . all things outside of Arkansas" was the Arkansawyer's most distinguishing trait. Borrowing one of H. L. Mencken's hyperbolic statements, Edson stated that not only had Arkansas failed to produce any first-rate scholars, but that no man of first-class intellect had ever been born there, or even passed through the state! The only real assets the author could discern in Arkansas were its splendid natural beauty and the people's native wit. As for certain claims set forth in booster literature such as the *Congressional Record* information sheet, Edson had these remarks:

What then does he [the Arkansas resident] glory in? He's a joiner of high-sounding, meaningless societies. He prides himself in the fact that "Albert Pike, America's most illustrious Mason, reached the zenith of his career while a resident of Arkansas," and that "the poet laureate of Masonry, Fay Hempstead, is a native Arkansan," and that "the only man ever invited to speak before the New York Lodge of Elks, not a member of the lodge, was an Arkansan."[25]

Naturally, Brough in his booster speeches added Edson and Mencken to the list of maligners of Arkansas whose "miserable diatribes" had to be refuted. In an address to some business leaders of Kansas City and Little Rock in 1924 he denounced the vilifiers and suggested that people who came to the state could see for themselves the multitude of good things about the Wonder State—including a "salubrious climate" and "cultured, God-fearing citizenship." Brough's correspondence in the mid-1920s reveals that in addition to his work for the Arkansas Advancement Association he served as director of the Arkansas Public Service Information Bureau, apparently an agency organized and funded by public utility interests in Arkansas. He assumed this position late in 1925, succeeding Earle Hodges, his old political rival (and friend!). Apparently the APSIB duties were about the same as the promotional work for Pettie's organization; for example, he prepared a lengthy—and of course, optimistic—article on Arkansas's business outlook in 1926, published in the *Arkansas Utility News.* His Arkansas-boosting was not restricted to those years in which he was under contract with the Advancement Association and the APSIB; in both his writing and oratory he continued in his role as defender and promoter of both Arkansas and the "New South." In an *Arkansas Democrat* article he saluted the New South's "broad-visioned political philosophers, constitutional lawyers and fascinating political leaders," and in a radio speech (KMOX, St. Louis) he boasted that Arkansas's "ministers, statesmen, lawyers . . . and other professional men and women" were worthy of the South's best cultural traditions. In the radio speech and elsewhere he provided his usual long list of positive facts about the state, sometimes including the fact that a "pure stream of Anglo-Saxon blood" flowed through the veins of most Arkansas residents.[26]

Brough and other Arkansas leaders remained alert to detractors of Arkansas and its people; for example, when an article in *Collier's Weekly* (December 1929) contained uncomplimentary remarks about Arkansas's late senator James P. Clarke, Brough wrote a lengthy open letter to the editor and asked for a retraction of the unfavorable publicity. He enclosed a copy of the radio address noted above, and asked both the letter and extracts of the speech be published. This was not done, although in a late March issue (1930), the editors stated their regrets that the December article had given an unfair picture of Clarke, and noted that the latter had been a "cultured and right honorable gentleman."[27]

Arkansas, like the whole nation, entered a period of hard times with the advent of the Great Depression. Actually, declining farm prices had brought hard times to Arkansas farmers throughout most of the twenties, and the onset of the depression brought an intensification of their suffering. Moreover, in the late twenties and early thirties, flood, tornadoes, and drought contributed to their plight. Arkansas problems were highlighted in a *Literary Digest* article in February 1931. Entitled "Arkansas's Fight for Life," the article painted a stark picture of a

> land of dusty desolation, sucked dry by the drought, rasped by the sharp edges of a cruel economic fate, her citizens destitute, hungry, and helpless.[28]

The *Literary Digest* article was sympathetic and presented a bright side: "Many observers believe that the worst of the ordeal is over." However, Arkansas's most notorious nemesis, H. L. Mencken, offered an analysis of the situation which once again roused the fury of Brough and other defenders and boosters of the state's good name. Mencken wrote in the *Baltimore Sun* (January and February 1931) that depression conditions in Arkansas were a shade worse than elsewhere because Arkansas was perhaps the most backward state in the Union, with only Mississippi offering it serious rivalry for last place in all statistical tables. Two-thirds of Arkansas citizens, he asserted, were benighted and miserable, and were preyed upon by politicians and preachers. Mencken feared that "not even the Red Cross, with all its munificence, could prevent the inhabitants from starving to death through congenital stupidity." Some parts of the state were so backward, he wrote, that children went naked till they were ten years of age and frequently lived in trees. Arkansas reacted to Mencken's attack swiftly and indignantly: the Arkansas legislature passed a resolution condemning both Mencken and his January article, and Dallas T. Herndon, director of the state archives, joined with Dr. Brough in a letter of protest addressed to the editor of the *Sun*. The letter was published in the *Sun* on February 10, and included in the House of Representatives *Journal* of 1931.[29]

Brough must have been the principal author of the letter, for in the first paragraph he refers to his postgraduate studies at the Johns Hopkins University, when he read the *Sun*, a "great newspaper. . . ." Responding to Mencken's prediction that Arkansas citizens would continue to be dependent upon the rest of the nation for relief of hunger, Brough asserted that except for 1927 and 1931, Arkansas—"the twin sister of Michigan in the galaxy of American states"—had never called on the nation as a whole for help, despite the calamities visited upon it by both the weather and economic depression.[30]

Answering Mencken's slur about the stupidity of Arkansas people, Brough pointed out that over two hundred Arkansans were listed in *Who's Who in America* and provided statistics on the state's educational accomplishments. He also boasted that over one hundred Arkansas writers had "achieved more than a local reputation"—and furnished a number of specific names. The letter went on to provide examples of accomplished Arkansans in politics, medicine, the ministry, and journalism and concluded with a demand that Mencken "should publicly apologize to the people whom he [had] so cruelly and wantonly maligned."[31]

Mencken's reply appeared in his column a few days later. After complimenting Brough as "the most learned Arkansan ever heard of," the sage summarily dismissed Brough's (and Herndon's) list of accomplished Arkansas citizens as "really too dreadful to be treated seriously." Moreover, he challenged Brough's claim that Arkansas was the "twin-sister of Michigan" among the states, pointing out that the former commonwealth did not compare favorably with Michigan in taxes paid, value of farmland, et cetera. In fact, he noted that the only areas in which Arkansas had a high ranking among the states was in the number of lynchings and prohibitionists. Mencken concluded that Brough failed, though honorably, "as a defender of the Arkansas *Kultur.*" Nonetheless, Brough persisted in his dispute with the journalist, penning a lengthy reply. He wrote that "the people of Arkansas do not care to engage in a controversy with you, for you have agencies of publicity which we have not." Nonetheless, he expressed regret that Mencken insisted on using his brilliant pen in the ignoble task of maligning Arkansas. Then Brough proceeded to do what he had often done before: identify and praise Arkansas citizens of note, including poets and businessmen. (Among the latter was a native Arkansan who had become "the highest paid auditor in the world.") Mencken's reaction indicated he was not moved; he continued to regard Arkansas as in a race with Mississippi for last place in most economic and cultural categories.[32]

Despite their war of words in the columns of the *Baltimore Sun,* Mencken and Brough respected each other. Mencken was flattered by Brough's request that he autograph some copies of *American Mercury,* and he solicited the Arkansan's assistance in gathering materials for a series of articles. Moreover, not all of the sage's comments on Arkansas were uncomplimentary; in a handwritten postscript to a note to Brough he described the Pine Bluff High School newspaper, which Brough had sent him, as "really excellent." He thought "it would be hard to find a better school paper" than the *Pine Cone*.[33]

Mencken appears to have wearied of "Arkansas bashing" after 1931, but other writers took up their cudgels—such as Travis Y. Oliver of El Dorado, whose article "Hell's Fire—Arkansas!" (*Vanity Fair*, 1933) claimed that Nature had blessed Arkansas "in everything except her citizens." In the tradition of C. L. Edson a decade earlier, Oliver paid tribute to the state's unsurpassed scenery and agricultural and mineral resources, but emphasized the "dearth of first raters" among Arkansas politicians, businessmen, writers, et cetera. Despite progress in transportation and increased funding for schools, the state continued to rank "low in all the finer forms of human endeavor." Oliver suggested that a principal reason was the pervasive influence of Fundamentalist preachers who diligently guard against new ideas. Of course, Oliver was added to the maligners of Arkansas whose attacks had to be refuted by Brough and others.[34]

Brough wrote to Miss Claire Boothe Brokaw, *Vanity Fair*'s managing editor, protesting Oliver's "libelous article" and requesting her to publish his enclosed reply. As he had done in his earlier joust with Mencken, Brough provided a long list of accomplished Arkansans, in a refutation of Oliver's charge that the state lacked "first raters." According to the recollections of Richard C. Butler, who at the time was a young lawyer in the Little Rock offices of Robinson, House, and Moses, Brough "borrowed" the firm's secretary for typing the letter to Miss Brokaw. Butler remembers that Brough, a long-time friend and associate of the senior members, paced back and forth, smoking cigarettes, while dictating the letter. The editor replied a few days later, indicating she would publish at least part of his reply to Oliver's article. Brough responded expressing his appreciation and sent her a copy of a poem by Albert Pike and a copy of Fred W. Allsopp's recently published book on Arkansas poetry. Brough indicated he was aware of the editor's space problems, but urged her to stress the "most important names" in his response to Oliver. He then added "such as" and identified some thirty names he had included in his list.[35]

The pattern of attack-and-defense continued beyond the lifetime of Brough, Mencken, and Oliver; the "image problem" has hardly been laid to rest. Evidences of this include the sensational media coverage of the Little Rock integration crisis and the "prison scandals" of the Faubus-Rockefeller era, and more recently, the anti-Arkansas sniping which accompanied Bill Clinton's emergence in national politics. Arkansas citizens continue to be called on to answer detractors and talk up the positive aspects of life in the Land of Opportunity. To date, no other Arkansas booster has taken up the task with as much energy, eloquence, and determination as characterized the efforts of Charles Hillman Brough.

CHAPTER 7

College President, University Booster

ESPITE HIS GRADUAL RECOVERY of health in the mid-1920s, Brough did not resume his customary vigorous schedule of promoting Arkansas and traveling the chautauqua and lyceum circuits. Instead, he returned to higher education—not as a professor, but as president of Central Baptist College in Conway. As he assumed that position in 1928, he did not realize that he would soon become embroiled in bitter controversy resulting from his stand on such issues as prohibition, anti-Catholicism, and evolution.

Brough had taken steps to re-enter the field of education three years earlier, accepting a position as educational secretary for both Central and Ouachita Baptist College in Arkadelphia. He had hoped to exert plenty of energy in this new responsibility *in addition to* his Arkansas boosting and chautauqua assignments. However, as we have seen, a breakdown in health curtailed all of these activities for over a year. It was not until August 1926, following extended periods of recuperation in Michigan and North Carolina, that he felt ready to resume at least some of his duties. Even then friends admonished him not to rush into his work too strenuously; one of them wrote, "You must lasso yourself . . . , or, elect Mrs. Brough boss and let her hold the reins."[1]

The phasing-out of Brough's chautauqua and lyceum career coincided with the decline of these institutions after 1925. As for his role as educational secretary for the two Baptist colleges, he apparently never really got started. However, he was able, either late in 1925 or early in 1926, to do some work as director of the Arkansas Public Services Information Bureau, writing and publishing a lengthy and optimistic assessment of the state's business outlook. Meanwhile, he continued to serve as vice-president of the Arkansas

Advancement Association. Brough was also available in 1926 to deliver addresses for special meetings—such as the Boy Scouts Executives' conference at Hot Springs, a Mississippi College celebration, and a chamber of commerce meeting in Conway.[2]

Writing to a friend in October, Brough told of his continued progress toward overcoming his "nervous affection." He credited Anne with seeing him through his long period of illness, but noted that she was not at all well and needed rest to restore her usual health and strength. Her condition was largely attributable to the death of her mother some weeks earlier, which had been a great shock to both Anne and Hillman. He observed that his wife had "certainly been through a siege," but was "bearing up nobly."[3]

Partly for further rest and recovery, the Broughs traveled to Europe in the spring and summer of 1927. They joined a tour conducted by Prof. Signor Marinoni of the University of Arkansas, leaving Little Rock in mid-June. They departed Montreal late in June on a Cunard liner and for about two months visited England, France, Germany, Switzerland, Belgium, and Italy. Brough believed the "treasures of art and sculpture" they saw made the trip "thoroughly worthwhile," and he was also impressed with the scenic beauty of various countries—although he asserted that he did not see any nation that could compare in all respects with Arkansas. He and Anne were fortunate in getting to attend sessions of the British Parliament, thanks to their good friend Sen. Joe T. Robinson, who had influence with the U.S. State Department.[4]

In taking the European trip, regrettably, they missed the graduation of Charlie, Knight's son, from Tulane. Following their return to Little Rock in September, Brough mailed "small remembrances" to Knight, Charlie, and his stepmother, Cora, in Los Angeles. He wrote Cora that both he and Anne returned from the trip "invigorated in health and strength." Brough gave a talk to the Authors and Composers Society, based on the European tour; and the Little Rock Lions Club hosted a luncheon in their honor. Getting news of this affair, Brough's one-time political foe Earl Hodges, living in New York City, wrote Brough a letter. Hodges told him, ". . . your friends in Arkansas and your scope of usefulness each increase as the years go by." Hodges had been pleased at the good news of Brough's improved health and at the reports of the good work he was doing with the information bureau.[5]

In April 1928 the resignation of Dr. Doak S. Campbell from the presidency of Central College in Conway provided Brough an opportunity to re-enter the field of higher education. Central, a Baptist junior college for girls, was under the direction of the Arkansas Baptist Convention. Three years earlier Brough had been "all set" to work for both Central and Ouachita as publicity agent, but as we have seen, his illness interrupted that activity. Brough, who delivered the commencement address to the 1928 class, was soon reported to be among the applicants the board of trustees was considering for the presidency. Apparently he was offered the job sometime in June; in a letter to a friend in Memphis he wrote that the "Conway people are very anxious for me to accept." He added that he felt sure he would accept, since his health was much improved and he was looking forward to getting back into educational work. In early July it was announced that Brough had been unanimously elected by the Central Board of Trustees. His salary was set at five thousand dollars a year, plus living expenses for himself and Mrs. Brough, who assumed the position of dean of women. Brough's job as president would consist mostly of recruiting and fund raising; administrative work would be primarily the responsibility of the dean of the college. Prior to the opening of the fall semester the Broughs moved into an apartment in Bruce Hall, a dormitory on campus.[6]

Brough received dozens of congratulatory letters; for example, from an associate justice of the state supreme court, a superintendent of education, a Baptist pastor in Memphis, and Virgil Pettie (manager of the state chamber of commerce). Of course, many letters of both congratulations and welcome were from Conway residents, for he had a host of friends there. He received cordial welcomes from the business and civic leaders, including the mayor. One of the most exuberant letters was from a faculty member at the Arkansas State Teachers College, who wrote:

> Welcome a thousand times to our little city! Central College is to be congratulated on securing your services and Conway is proud to have you and your fine wife become citizens of this fine little town.[7]

Brough's predecessor at Central, Doak Campbell, spoke at Brough's inauguration in September, comparing the new executive with Robert E. Lee in dedication to the cause of higher education. At Central's opening session the new president asserted his support of high academic standards and pledged to work diligently to raise a permanent endowment for the college. He further promised that if such a fund were raised, he and Mrs. Brough would give the school their library of over five thousand volumes.[8]

Receptions honoring the Broughs included one hosted by the Conway Chamber of Commerce at the Hendrix College gymnasium. Joining the honorees in the receiving line were President and Mrs. John Hugh Reynolds of Hendrix College, President and Mrs. B. W. Torreyson of the State Teachers College, and Jo Frauenthal, president of the chamber of commerce. Frauenthal predicted the Broughs would enjoy many happy and useful years in the congenial environment of Conway.[9]

Certainly both Central College and Conway were congenial enough. The new president may have experienced a pleasant sense of *deja vu* in coming to Central, since some of his fondest memories from the Clinton years were at Hillman College (previously Central Female Institute). And considering his consistent support of Christian education and his long-time active involvement in the Baptist church, it would seem there would be little prospect of his tenure at Central leading to any sort of controversy. However, Brough's year at Conway, while on the whole happy and useful, was far from tranquil; in the fall of 1928 he became embroiled in a bitter feud with influential Baptist leaders —not local churchmen, but prominent leaders of the state convention.[10]

The controversy stemmed from the presidential campaign of 1928. Brough, always a staunch Democrat, predictably was strongly in favor of his party's ticket: Gov. Al Smith of New York and his running mate, Sen. Joe T. Robinson of Arkansas, whom Brough had nominated for president in 1924. While he did not endorse Governor Smith's "erratic views on the liquor question," Brough heartily supported his progressivism and regarded him as ". . . the most magnetic personality of our day and an able, constructive, fearless statesman." But the "liquor question" led many Protestant ministers and editors, especially in the South, to denounce the Democratic ticket. In addition, the fact that Smith was Catholic provoked widespread Protestant opposition.[11]

In previous presidential contests Brough had made many political speeches under the auspices of the Democratic party Speakers' Bureau, but in 1928 he declined a regular assignment with the bureau. Writing to the chairman he pointed out that his duties as college president made extensive political speechmaking impossible, although in September he did deliver a number of such addresses, including several in Oklahoma and Alabama, as well as in Arkansas.[12]

Brough's public support of the Smith-Robinson ticket immediately drew sharp criticism from Baptist leaders opposed to Smith. Responding to their attacks, Brough in a speech to a special session of the Arkansas legislature charged that "political divines" were betraying the South to the Republican party. Brough's position was in essential agreement with a lawyer friend who wrote him regarding "many of our preachers who ought to be sticking to the Word [but who] have converted their pulpits into political platforms to denounce the Democratic ticket. . . ."[13]

Brough's remarks about political divines produced further criticism from Baptist leaders, including Dr. J. S. Compere, editor of the denomination's statewide publication, the *Baptist Advance*. Compere reported that many readers had sent him letters protesting Brough's statements. One of these letters was actually a copy of one which a disgruntled Baptist preacher had written to Brough. Compere quoted extensively from it, including the following passage:

> I am a friend to Central College. I have put my money into it. My oldest daughter was graduated there. I regret that the president of Central College has chosen to publicly dub as "Political divines" the Baptist preachers of Arkansas who have largely made possible Central College, because their convictions compel them to speak out in one of the greatest crises that has ever confronted the American people.

The writer claimed that in supporting Hoover over Smith he was in company with prominent clergymen such as Bishop Cannon as well as at least 95 percent of all evangelical preachers in the South, plus "... the awakened motherhood of America, the National WCTU and Anti-Saloon League," and all the organized moral forces in the country.[14]

In the same issue of the *Advance* Compere noted that although Brough had the right to support the candidate of his choice, it was out of place for a man in his responsible position to go directly counter to the declared policy of the Arkansas Baptist Convention. (In 1927 the convention had adopted a resolution placing the church on record as against any presidential candidate opposed to the Eighteenth [Prohibition] Amendment.) In a later issue Compere observed that preachers were called by God, then asked, "Who calls the preaching politician,—the politician who preaches to the preachers and tells them to keep their mouths shut about the great moral issues that are before us ...?"[15]

In addition to speeches, Brough aired his political views in the *Arkansas Gazette*. Responding to a request by the Woman's Page editor, he set forth his reasons for supporting the Smith-Robinson ticket. One of the reasons pertained to the fact that much of the opposition to Governor Smith was based on his Catholic faith. Brough believed that the election of Smith would prove a death blow to such religious intolerance. He further noted that it was a Baptist preacher, Roger Williams, who first proclaimed the principles of religious freedom and the absolute separation of church and state.[16]

The feud between Brough and his Baptist critics reached a climax late in October. Brough was scheduled to address a Democratic rally in El Dorado on October 27. On that date, in an attempt to prevent him from speaking, Compere and Dr. J. S. Rogers, executive secretary of the state convention, sent him a telegram of warning. Because Brough was president of an institution of the convention, they strongly protested against his speaking that night contrary to the convention's official position on "wet" presidential candidates. The telegram closed as follows: "We solemnly warn you that we believe our people and the Convention will not stand for it."[17]

In angry defiance of this warning Brough proceeded to deliver his speech at El Dorado and told his audience about the effort to silence him. He characterized the Compere-Rogers telegram as "one of the most flagrant" attempts at coercion he had encountered in his public career. Brough denounced the authors for presuming to dictate to a former governor in political matters and evoked an outburst of applause from the audience by appealing to their enthusiasm for Robinson as the vice-presidential candidate. He charged the *Baptist Advance* with becoming an organ for the Republicans and certain Baptist preachers with converting their pulpits into pro-Hoover rostrums. He reiterated a point made in the *Arkansas Gazette* interview—that the election of Al Smith would be a great blow against religious tolerance. (Although the warning telegram from Compere and Rogers did not mention religion, Brough was convinced that these men, and many other anti-Smith Baptists, were more concerned about the candidate's Catholicism than his position on prohibition.) Brough's speech received front-page coverage in the next day's issue of the *El Dorado Sunday News,* with a streamer headline: "Brough Defies the Church."[18]

Actually, Brough's challenge was directed mainly at Compere and Rogers, for there were many Baptists who sided with him following the El Dorado episode. For several days after the El Dorado speech he received scores of supportive telegrams and letters. One of these was from Virgil Pettie, who congratulated the embattled educator for the "very fine, dignified and forceful manner" in which he replied to certain church leaders. Pettie added,

> It is inconceivable that any large percentage of the members of the Baptist Church would hold the same viewpoint as apparently held by Messrs. Compere and Rogers.

University of Arkansas president John Futrall expressed the same sentiments, and assured Brough that "the thing has redounded very greatly to your credit and glory." One telegram was from a group of supporters from the El Dorado area, telling of a huge Democratic rally at which Brough's "moral courage and political integrity" were endorsed.[19]

Similar messages of support came from Fayetteville, Monticello, Brinkley, and many other parts of the state. Gratified by these endorsements, Brough delivered another series of political speeches, in which he continued to denounce religious intolerance and efforts of "Baptist popes" to muzzle him.

Brough wrote many letters of appreciation to those who wrote him uphold-ing his defiance of the Rogers-Compere group. Following is an excerpt from a representative reply from Brough:

> Words are inadequate to express to you my heart-felt appreciation of your splendid reassuring message commending me for the traditional Baptist stand for independence of thought and speech I took at El Dorado.... I wish you would tell all my friends and every loyal Democrat you see ... that the reac-tion from this incident of our state campaign has been very favorable all over Arkansas and that I believe it will contribute something to the glorious vic-tory we will win in Arkansas, and I believe in the nation, on November the sixth.[20]

Although the Democratic ticket was buried in Hoover's landslide win, Smith and Robinson *did* carry Arkansas, while losing several other southern states. Important to the Arkansas victory were Robinson's popularity as a "native son" and Brough's crusade against religious bigotry. It should be noted that the latter's liberal position on religion and freedom of expression was balanced by his appeal to anti-Negro sentiment during the campaign. In speeches and letters he extolled white supremacy and charged that it was threatened by the prospect of Republican inroads in the "Solid South." An anti-Hoover political advertisement in one of the Brough-Roark scrapbooks tells of a white woman's visit to the offices of the commerce department in Washington (Hoover was head of that department). The woman saw "white girls being compelled to work alongside desks with negro men and using rest rooms with negro girls." Some months following the Hoover victory Brough wrote to Arkansas's senator Thaddeus Caraway, thanking him for

> calling attention of the Nation to the fact that the wife of a negro congress-man was entertained at a White House tea.[21]

During the presidential campaign Brough came under fire from fellow Baptists over another controversial issue—an anti-evolution bill which would be decided on by Arkansas voters in the November election. The bill proposed to make it unlawful for public schools to teach that "mankind ascended or descended from a lower order of animals." Brough and other men of statewide influence—such as ex-governor McRae, President Reynolds of Hendrix, and President Futrall of the University of Arkansas—took a public stand against the measure. In a letter to a Presbyterian clergyman who also opposed it, Brough indicated he thought it unwise to enact laws on controversial scientific and religious questions. Stating his personal belief in theistic evolution, he strongly opposed any legislation designed to thwart scientific research.[22]

In 1924 the state Baptist convention had passed resolutions which unequiv-ocally reaffirmed the Genesis account of creation and rejected evolutionary theories, including theistic evolution. The resolutions further required that all teachers and other employees of Baptist schools sign a copy of the reso-lutions. It is doubtful that Brough conformed to this requirement, since he took a public position of opposition to the initiated bill against evolution in the public schools. And this position seemed, to his critics, another example of his disrespect for the church's teachings and policies. In the *Baptist Advance* of November 1—shortly after the brouhaha over the El Dorado speech—Compere published a letter from a Fundamentalist Baptist preacher who said that he doubted that "Brough and Broughism" at Central would continue to be tolerated by Arkansas Baptists. In the same issue Compere hinted that in view of Brough's disregard of the church's doctrine on evolution, he might be expected to embrace other heresies and indicated there was reason to sus-pect him of believing in open communion.[23]

The results of the November 6 election were as gratifying to the Compere-Rogers group as they were disappointing to Brough and his allies. Added to Hoover's resounding victory was the Arkansas voters' approval, by a sizable majority, of the bill forbidding the teaching of evolution in the public schools. But the feud between Brough and his critics was not necessarily over. There was a good chance that the rancor which had developed would produce a showdown at the state Baptist convention, scheduled to open at Texarkana on November 20. Brough suspected that Compere and Rogers were plotting to gain control of the convention and then get some of their partisans elected to the Central Board of Trustees. If such a plot succeeded, an anti-Brough majority of the board could force the president to resign.[24]

To head off such an indirect attack, Brough fired off a number of letters to Baptist friends throughout the state, beseeching them to exert their influence to get open-minded delegates, or messengers, sent to the Texarkana gathering. The following excerpt from a letter to a Lonoke minister is repre-sentative:

> Please mobilize all the Baptist forces of Lonoke, Prairie, and Monroe counties, where you are so favorably known, and see to it that messengers are sent from the various churches . . . who will keep an open mind on all controverted propositions and will not do the bidding of Rogers and Compere.[25]

About a week before the convention opened Brough joined Compere and Rogers in a conciliatory statement published in the *Advance*. And there was no "showdown" on the floor of the convention regarding the controversies over either the pro-Smith speeches or the evolution issue. However, in a "behind the scenes" compromise, Brough agreed to comply with the convention's requirement that its employees sign the 1924 resolutions concerning evolution. In signing, Brough insisted that he was merely indicating that he did not believe man was descended from an anthropoid ape. This conformed to the recently passed law regarding the public schools, but hardly constituted full acceptance of the church's doctrine, which was rejection of evolution in any form. To re-emphasize its unbending position the 1928 convention adopted a resolution *reaffirming* its 1924 statements. Thus Brough's more liberal view was clearly rejected.[26]

The *Gazette* reported that the convention had ended harmoniously. But early in January Brough, in a speech at Dallas, again blasted ministers who preached politics from their pulpits. Compere, who had announced he was soon leaving the editorship of the *Advance,* was predictably angry at Brough's remarks, and urged readers to protest them by writing both to Brough and to the Central Board of Trustees. In March Brough submitted his resignation as president—to take effect immediately—and the board accepted. Two months later they hired Dr. Rogers as his successor. These developments suggest that Brough's fears of a plot to oust him had materialized; however, there is insufficient evidence for this conclusion. Brough's announced reason for quitting the presidency was the offer of a job with the University of Arkansas, as special publicity agent. The Broughs retained their Bruce Hall apartment until the end of the semester, since Mrs. Brough, at the request of the board, agreed to continue as dean of women through that period.[27]

After accepting Brough's resignation, the Central Board of Trustees announced their regret at losing their president and expressed their appreciation of Brough's services in popularizing the college and securing substantial donations for the school's maintenance fund. The board's statement also pointed out that he was leaving "with the best wishes of the Board of Trustees, the faculty, and the student body, for success in his new work." The entire faculty signed a statement of appreciation to the outgoing president. They assured him that he had ". . . won their hearts by his noble bearing, his Christian spirit, his gentle kindness, his gracious courtesy, and his delightful addresses." In addition, every student signed her name to a statement regretting his resignation and thanking him for his "untiring interest" in their welfare.[28]

The *Centralian* described the new duties of the departing "beloved president": promotion of the University of Arkansas through public speeches, organizing local alumni associations, securing contributions to a scholarship fund, assisting in the promotion of the extension program. Among the congratulatory messages Brough received was one from Senator Robinson, who expressed confidence that he would render valuable service to the university due to his popularity throughout the state.[29]

Brough's new job, like his various other positions since leaving the governor's office, involved much speechmaking, both from the lecture platform and over the radio. Some of his speeches were published; following is an excerpt from a 1929 address which appeared in the *Arkansas Democrat:*

> Arkansas can never become great educationally when the false propaganda spreads abroad that Arkansas schools are not up to the standard and that we rank at the bottom of the ladder among the states of the Union in our educational advantages and equipment.

He went on to point out that Arkansas was actually thirty-seventh in the condition of its public school system and near the top of the southern states in the standard of its higher institutions of learning. He elaborated on the educational progress over the previous twenty-five years and expressed regret that many Arkansas parents tended to patronize out-of-state schools.[30]

Brough's audiences included high-school graduating classes; reporting to President Futrall in June 1929 he wrote that he had delivered approximately twenty-five such speeches. He also addressed college groups, teachers' institutes, and civic organizations. He delivered a number of addresses over the radio; for example, a 1929 broadcast over station KMOX in St. Louis and a series of weekly talks over station KTHS in Hot Springs. In the KMOX address he lauded the university and its president, John Futrall, as well as Arkansas's public schools, the state teachers' colleges, the denominational institutions, the newly established Crescent College at Eureka Springs, and various other aspects of life in the Wonder State. Since this more general boosting—joined with his promotion of the university—characterized many of his speeches during the 1929–32 period, it is difficult in some cases to determine whether he was carrying out his specific duties for the university.[31]

Although Brough plunged into his promotional work with his accustomed vigor and enthusiasm, he and Anne did manage to take a vacation at Lake Lucerne, near Eureka Springs, in the summer of 1929. With Anne driving, and with Hillman's stepmother, Cora Brough, with them, they motored to Fayetteville late in June. While there they attended a wedding and visited with friends, and Dr. Brough delivered an address to the annual meeting of the Arkansas Press Association. On June 29 Cora departed for Los Angeles, and Hillman and Anne continued to Eureka Springs.[32]

Later that year the Broughs were saddened by two deaths: In early

September Granville Roark's father-in-law, H. L. Price, a Fayetteville business-man, died suddenly; a few days later Knight's wife, Fannie, died in Vicksburg. Brough wrote a brief tribute to Mr. Price, then rushed to Vicksburg to be with Knight and Fannie as the latter lay on her deathbed.[33]

In addition to speechmaking during this period Brough published sev-eral articles; for example, in the first months of his work as special publicity representative he wrote an article for the *Arkansas Democrat* and had an inter-view published in the *Hot Springs Centennial Record,* on the problem of Arkansas youth leaving the state for their higher education. Another of Brough's articles was a more general one on the University of Arkansas. It appeared in the official publication of the Knights of Pythias, one of whose officers wrote to Futrall commending Brough and assuring the university president that the favorable publicity would be widely disseminated. Brough was undeniably interested in the dissemination of his writings and wrote let-ters to various newspaper editors asking them to reproduce articles, or at least their substance, which had appeared in other papers.[34]

One of Brough's strategies for strengthening the university was to mar-shal university alumni in support of their alma mater. Shortly after taking the job as special publicity representative he began writing alumni asking them to submit names of other former students and alumni in their county. Through this correspondence and personal visits he wished to lay the foun-dation for local alumni clubs and later to solicit from them donations to scholarships and student loan funds. In a letter to President Futrall describ-ing progress on these and other activities, Brough reported that everywhere he went he found the situation "very flattering" for the university.[35]

As noted above, Brough's oratory during this period covered a diversity of topics and was delivered to a variety of audiences. He spoke to local chau-tauquas, high-school graduating classes, college convocations, teachers' insti-tutes, and women's groups and presented radio broadcasts as well as lectures in person. Among the themes which received especially prominent coverage in the press were the depression and politics. Discussing the economic con-ditions of Arkansas around 1930, he tempered his customary optimism as he sketched the plight of farmers, businessmen, unemployed workers, and others. However, he was confident that both the region and his state possessed the "civic courage" to weather the crisis. As seen in an earlier chapter, Brough (and other Arkansas leaders) sprang to the defense of Arkansas against H. L. Mencken and other critics. As for the national economic scene, his advocacy of a billion-dollar road-building program by the federal government drew banner headlines in a Monroe (Louisiana) newspaper. Brough believed that such a mammoth public works program would provide relief for the unemployed as well as a ten-thousand-mile network of federal roads.[36]

Brough did not neglect criticizing the policies of the Hoover administration (as well as the preceding Republican regimes). He was particularly sharp in his criticism of the high tariff schedules of the Hawley-Smoot Act. Like Democrats everywhere, Brough anticipated Democratic victory in the 1932 presidential election. As might be expected, he promoted Senator Robinson for the party nomination; in November 1929 he led in the organization of a "Robinson for President" club, and in speeches delivered in 1930 predicted Robinson would be the next president of the United States. Many other Arkansas Democrats agreed, and in 1930 the Democratic State Convention unanimously endorsed Robinson for president. Brough seconded the nomination, and then startled the delegates in his report of comments he had heard recently from prominent eastern Democrats. He said that Gov. Franklin D. Roosevelt of New York had said that if he could not obtain the Democratic nomination for president in 1932, that there was no man he would rather support than Senator Robinson. Brough reported also that Maryland governor Albert C. Ritchie had expressed, through a spokesman, that if he failed to be nominated he would put his strength behind Robinson. Upon learning of Brough's statements, Roosevelt, through his secretary, suggested the Arkansan had misinterpreted his remarks; the New York governor had merely expressed warm regard for Senator Robinson. Ritchie's spokesman, a Maryland judge, stated that Brough's assertion regarding Ritchie's commitment to Robinson was an "absurd untruth." Following these denials Brough conceded he might have drawn the wrong inferences from remarks made in his presence.[37]

As for any personal political ambitions, Brough in December 1930 insisted publicly that he had none at present. Instead, he intended to concentrate on his efforts in the cause of education in Arkansas and would steer clear of politics for the next two years. As things developed, his re-entry into politics occurred about eight months sooner than he had anticipated.[38]

CHAPTER 8

A Victim of the "Kingfish"

*T*HE REVIVAL OF BROUGH's political ambitions was precipitated by the death of Arkansas's junior senator Thaddeus Caraway on November 6, 1931. It was a kind of *deja vu* situation for Brough, who once again had to decide between working for the university and running for public office. Had Senator Caraway lived three days longer, Gov. Harvey Parnell could have appointed a successor to serve until the expiration of the term in 1933; however, under Arkansas law a special election would be necessary since the senator's death occurred more than a year prior to the next general election, November 8, 1932.[1]

The day after Caraway died, a Sheridan lawyer, Isaac McClellan, wrote Parnell, urging him to appoint Dr. Brough to serve until an election could be held. McClellan cited Brough's party loyalty and courage, especially as shown by his support of the Smith-Robinson ticket in 1928, in defiance of certain "high churchmen." Instead, the governor appointed Thaddeus Caraway's widow, Hattie, to serve as senator until the special election could be held. Parnell and other Democratic party leaders thought this an appropriately chivalrous arrangement; and although several of them were looking to seek the office in the August 1932 primary, they also decided that Mrs. Caraway should be the party's nominee for the special election, which Governor Parnell scheduled for January 12.[2]

None of these politicians anticipated that Hattie would seek the regular party nomination in August; she was expected to retire after a few months as senator and allow the male politicians to battle among themselves for the nomination. None of these aspirants would have the advantage of incumbency; Mrs. Caraway would be the incumbent, but she would step aside.[3]

Since Arkansas was essentially a solidly Democratic state, Mrs. Caraway, as her party's nominee, was assured of victory in the special election. However,

Democrats did not wish to have voters lose interest in the race and were eager to have a respectable showing at the polls. To achieve this, the State Democratic Committee named a special committee of seven women who were charged especially with encouraging women to turn out for Hattie. She won the election easily, of course, polling 31,133 votes to fewer than 3,000 for the two independent candidates in the race.[4]

Early in February, Brough, who was on a speaking engagement in the East, paid his respects to Mrs. Caraway in Washington. Her journal records two visits by Brough on February 9 and 10, but provides no details except a note that he had introduced her to Will Rogers.[5]

Brough had continued to receive letters of encouragement with respect to the August primary. A Forrest City supporter assured him he was better known than any of the others expected to enter the race; a Memphis friend wrote him that the people of Arkansas owed him the office—they wished to repay him for selling Arkansas to the world. Florence B. Cotman issued a statement in which she claimed that "The women of Arkansas will welcome the opportunity to vote for Dr. Charles H. Brough. . . ." She cited his stand in favor of votes for women—using his influence to secure the state primary law of 1917 and summoning a special legislative session in 1919 for the purpose of ratifying Amendment Nineteen to the federal Constitution.[6]

Several days before he formally announced for the Democratic primary race for the Senate, a controversy erupted between Brough and his employer, the University of Arkansas—or, more precisely, between Brough and university president John Futrall. Brough was angered by a resolution adopted by the board of trustees barring university staff members from participating in politics. Brough believed the resolution was aimed at him, and that Futrall was behind it. Futrall denied that the resolution was aimed at anyone in particular, but claimed it was designed to keep political entanglements out of the university.[7]

Brough did not let the matter drop. He said that he had made it clear that if he decided to enter the Senate race he would resign his position as extension lecturer. He also reminded the public that he had been a consistent friend of the university; for example, he had pressed for the 1917 legislation establishing a millage for the university and had also secured better salaries for professors and administrators. True to his word, Brough resigned his position as lecturer prior to issuance of his formal announcement for the primary contest. Opening his campaign with a speech at Fayetteville on March 10, he attacked Futrall for imposing a "gag rule" and insinuated that the university president was overpaid—with a salary of ten thousand dollars and a substantial expense account.[8]

Why did he make such a big issue of the "gag rule" and dwell on his feud with Futrall, whom Brough had described in 1930 as "one of the ablest educational executives in the nation"? The available evidence does not afford an explanation. Perhaps there were other points of friction between the two men in addition to the clash over the board's resolution, or perhaps Brough saw a parallel between the current controversy and his dispute with Baptist leaders in 1928 and hoped that spotlighting his political courage would benefit him as he entered upon the race for the Senate nomination.[9]

In the Fayetteville speech Brough shifted from the tilt with Futrall to his platform for the contest at hand. His first point was an assertion that there was too much government in business and not enough business in government (a Coolidge-like statement, seemingly unprogressive and out of place in the depression years). He then denounced the Hawley-Smoot tariff and called for its repeal and for substitution of a common-sense tariff. Other parts of his platform included (1) abolition of the Federal Farm Board, which he pronounced a failure, or placing it under the direction of dirt farmers; (2) replacing the gold standard with bimetallism (Brough blamed the gold standard for many of the country's woes); (3) conservation of natural resources (here Brough lauded Harvey Couch, of Arkansas Power and Light Company, for his contributions); (4) federal aid for roadbuilding, which would create jobs as well as modernize transportation; and (5) a program of relief using commodities stored by the Federal Farm Board.[10]

After the March "kickoff" Brough received many more letters from friends all over Arkansas expressing delight that he had chosen to run, wishing him success, and assuring him that large numbers of voters would welcome the opportunity to repay him for his services to the state over the years. Some letters were from friends outside Arkansas; they were also encouraging and usually expressed regret at not being able to cast their ballots for him.[11]

Although Brough, in his campaign speeches, gave considerable attention to the program outlined in his opening address, he believed that he would win many votes because of his accomplishments as governor and for his years of effort to promote Arkansas and its resources. He wrote numerous letters to supporters urging them to enlighten (or remind) people in their communities regarding the former governor's qualifications—honesty, efficiency, training in economics—and his untiring labors to attract industry to Arkansas and to boost the state's image. Writing to Mr. and Mrs. J. S. Lake of De Queen, for example, he provided them with a "script" to use in talking up his candidacy:

> Dr. Brough has advertised Arkansas in every State of the Union for the past
> thirty years with the exception of four years, during which he served as the

World War Chief Executive of Arkansas. This advertising was done as a private citizen or as a member of the University staff.

Writing a Crossett educator, and supplying him with a similar "script," Brough noted that he had recently mailed out more than ten thousand brochures on "Arkansas, the Commonwealth of Opportunity and Achievement"—a long, detailed address which he had delivered over a St. Louis radio station. Brough vowed that if elected to the Senate he would prove diligent and capable in meeting his responsibilities, and would use the Senate as a kind of national platform to continue promoting Arkansas and its resources. Probably many Arkansans shared the views of a Tyronza doctor who wrote Brough as follows:

> You have done more good in advertising the state of Arkansas than all other men put together. We owe you a debt that we are going to partly pay this year.

Another supporter wrote, ". . . the people in the state owe to you the office and all you have got to do is ask for it."[12]

Although Brough knew the task was not quite *that* simple, he had good reasons to be very optimistic about his prospects. From the early stages, reports from his supporters throughout the state, his contacts with the voters, and popular response to his speechmaking caused him to view his victory as a foregone conclusion. The following comments, taken from letters to Brough and his campaign secretary, Benton Kitchens, are representative of the optimism of Brough's enthusiastic supporters:

> . . . you will be nominated to the United States Senate and . . . your vote [will] equal, or nearly so, the entire vote cast for all other candidates combined. . . .

> I never in all my life saw a man that has as many friends as you have, and it is all over the State the same way.

> I feel sure you are going to win with a big majority. I have talked to a great many people in all walks of life, and the universal opinion is that you are the winner.

> [writer is sending Brough a set of histories] . . . which I think you will enjoy reading between the date of the election and your departure for Washington.[13]

Some of the correspondents mentioned personal favors Brough had done for them or members of their families, as well as for the people of Arkansas in general. One lady recalled how good Brough had been to her and her father. Many writers focused on the candidate's character and ability; a Vandervoort man wrote,

We want men of vision; men of courage; and men of untarnished and solid integrity....

From Calico Rock came the assurance that "Arkansas knows that you came from the Governor's chair with a clean and efficient record and that you are eminently qualified in every way [for senator]." An article on Brough in the *Memphis Commercial Appeal,* one of a series on the seven candidates for the nomination, pointed out two of his principal political "weapons": his ability to remember names, and his "graciousness of manner." This latter trait was said to evoke "all the fine traditions of the old south...."[14]

Brough, by nature an optimist, was heartened by the cheerful reports which continued to come in. He believed that his political appeal equaled or surpassed that of 1916: "All of my old friends are still loyal," he wrote a Forrest City supporter, "and in addition, scores of prominent people who fought for me in the race of 1916 are actively supporting me." Late in May he received a report from a traveling man, "an impartial observer," that Brough's minimum vote would be 142,000—and only 62,000 were needed for the nomination! Moreover, he and Mrs. Brough had contacted political leaders, by voting precincts, in sixty-three of the seventy-five counties, and concluded that he was certain to carry fifty-nine of them.[15]

His confidence was tempered by the fact that certain candidates posed a challenge, especially O. L. Bodenhamer, an El Dorado businessman and former national commander of the American Legion. Surprisingly, Bodenhamer was *not* a staunch advocate of the veterans' "bonus," but he did have strong support from such organizations as the Legion and the Veterans of Foreign Wars. Two other opponents to be concerned about were William F. Kirby, an Arkansas supreme court justice, and Vincent M. Miles, who was popular in the Fort Smith area. The two remaining candidates drew very little support. None of these politicians expected the incumbent, Sen. Hattie Caraway, to file for the contest; and when she did so in May, her decision was viewed with puzzlement rather than with anxiety. Brough's supporters frequently apprised him of how successful his rivals were in attracting voters; for example, how well a candidate's speech went over, what the sentiment of a community was toward the respective candidates, and so on. Even after taking a careful account of the potential strengths of rivals, Brough, his wife, and his campaign staff (consisting mainly of secretary Benton Kitchens) felt sure of victory.[16]

Throughout the campaign Brough traveled an average of one thousand miles per week, eventually visiting seventy-four of the state's seventy-five counties, and delivered an average of two to four speeches per day. He gave about three hundred addresses, to audiences totaling about two hundred thousand. This regimen was reminiscent of his most active chautauqua period, although most of his chautauqua travels were by rail rather than automobile. The senatorial campaign was rigorous not only for the candidate—who apparently never learned to drive—but also for his driver, who was none other than Anne Brough! Having her at the wheel was in part an economy measure, for Brough had very limited financial resources (as in 1920, when he declined to run for the Senate because of the expense involved). Mrs. Brough contributed more to her husband's campaign than just driving the car; she possessed a "graciousness of manner" and was very personable and popular. She also contributed to the campaign by writing letters to women in various communities, soliciting their support for her husband. One of their friends observed in a letter that "Anne's work among the women was producing wonderful results."[17]

Anne's role as her husband's driver ended with an automobile accident on July 4, in which she suffered a broken shoulder. The accident occurred near Rector; the Broughs, Mr. and Mrs. Kitchens, and a Mrs. Ross McClerkin were en route to Piggot where Brough was to speak. The car ran into some loose gravel, and Mrs. McClerkin, who had "spelled" Anne at the wheel, lost control. The car plunged into a ditch and turned over, pinning the occupants beneath it. Mrs. McClerkin and her sister, Mrs. Kitchens, suffered minor injuries, but Dr. Brough and Mr. Kitchens were reported to be unhurt (although it was later discovered that the candidate had sustained a broken rib). Anne, who suffered the most serious injury, was hospitalized at Paragould for several days before being brought home to Little Rock.[18]

The day following the accident a story in the *Ozark Spectator* reported that Brough chartered an airplane in order to fill his remaining speaking engagements for the day, but a scrapbook clipping from an unidentified newspaper indicates that Mrs. Brough dissuaded him from this and that he canceled the engagements. A few days following the accident a newspaper story quoted Brough as saying Anne was resting well, and that she was chiefly concerned about being unable to continue to drive the car for the rest of the campaign. Meanwhile, Brough, with a substitute driver, was back on the campaign trail soon after the accident, advocating various actions for coping with the nation's economic crisis—bimetallism, repeal of the Smoot-Hawley tariff, reduction of federal expenditures by abolishing useless bureaus and commissions.[19]

Assurances from his supporters that he could expect an easy victory were especially pleasing in view of Brough's limited financial resources; he had to conduct a simple, inexpensive campaign. The Broughs covered the bulk of the campaign costs—mostly travel and advertising—by borrowing on paid-up life insurance and by mortgaging their home. Former students and other friends donated sums—mostly small—to pay for gasoline, motor oil, and other expenses. As they journeyed from county to county, they were frequently house guests of friends, thus reducing their travel expenses somewhat. Late in July some Little Rock friends, on their own initiative, rented space for a county headquarters, with no cost to the candidate, whose headquarters had previously been the Brough home on Arch Street.[20]

Considering the "shoe string" nature of his campaign, it was ironic that a rumor began to circulate concerning Brough's "slush fund" provided by special interests backing him. Perhaps his long-time association with Harvey Couch, Hamilton Moses, and Sen. Joe T. Robinson led some to believe the charge, but there is no evidence that any special interests were pushing his candidacy. They certainly did not provide him with campaign money; his total expenditures—for travel, advertising, staff, et cetera—amounted to $7,301.91. A judge introducing Brough at De Queen was probably correct when he said that if the former governor was elected he would go to the Senate "unhampered by special obligations and free to follow that course which [would] be to the best interests of his people." The judge added that Dr. Brough would be a "fitting successor to the matchless Caraway" (no doubt referring to the late Thaddeus rather than his widow, the incumbent).[21]

During the campaign another anti-Brough rumor arose: it said that he was in poor health and too old to serve effectively as senator. Brough and his supporters immediately sought to dispel the idea, both in speeches and in campaign advertising. At a Little Rock rally late in July, J. S. Utley pointed out that Dr. Brough had just turned fifty-six, and he reminded the crowd that Washington was fifty-seven when he first took the presidential oath, Jefferson was fifty-eight when he took the oath, and Jackson sixty-two. Brough himself had asserted that his health was fine; it had to be, he said, or he could not endure the rigorous pace he was following: an average of one thousand miles a week since March, and an average of two to four speeches a day. It is interesting to note, however, that pictures of him in campaign advertisements and flyers were from his gubernatorial days. Brough and his friends may have been attempting to convey an image of a more youthful candidate; or they may have been simply using old "cuts" to save time and money. The contrast between his appearance in 1918 and in 1932 was considerable and may have misled readers who had not seen the former governor in person for several years; yet for the thousands who saw and heard him in 1932, the signs of aging were probably offset by viewing him on the political platform with apparently the vigor and energy of his chautauqua days. (Once, during the campaign, he grew incoherent and made a poor showing, but that one incident probably did not cause many voters to conclude he was unfit to serve.)[22]

As noted previously, Brough and his staff received periodic reports on the other candidates, particularly Miles and Bodenhamer, who were conceded to have a burgeoning of support in certain sections of the state. However, neither Brough nor the other male politicians in the race gave much attention to the somewhat belated candidacy of the incumbent, Sen. Hattie Caraway. When Hattie filed for the primary election on May 9, the news seemed to have evoked bemusement rather than apprehension among the other contenders. Few gave her serious consideration, and many believed she would be fortunate to get 3,000 of the expected 250,000 votes. A letter from a Marianna supporter said her friends there were surprised at the announcement of her candidacy and indicated they had the impression she did not wish to enter the race. The same citizen, responding to Mrs. Caraway's request for a frank assessment of the "political situation," characterized her chances of success as negligible.[23]

Mrs. Caraway, like Dr. Brough, had insufficient resources for financing a campaign. However, a fellow senator, Huey P. Long of Louisiana, had the funds and the "know how"—and willingness—to help her succeed. On July 19, three weeks from election day, Mrs. Caraway formally accepted Long's offer to enter Arkansas and conduct an intensive one-week campaign on her behalf. She explained that she and the Louisiana senator were on the same side on a number of issues which came before the Senate, and that they were both independent-minded in their voting, committed to vote for the masses rather than for special interests. Until August 1, when she was to meet the "Kingfish" at Magnolia to launch their joint six-day speaking tour, Senator Caraway was on her own. Regarding her first campaign speech, a radio address over KTHS (Hot Springs), she said it would be "my first, really honest-to-goodness speech in my whole life."[24]

One of the reasons Long decided to "invade" Arkansas was to enhance his prestige and demonstrate that his political strength extended beyond Louisiana. Another was that he and Mrs. Caraway had voted the same way on a number of bills before the Senate. The Arkansas lawmaker evidently shared the progressive outlook of the "Kingfish," and was willing to stand up to the conservatives, whom Long accused of being controlled by special interests—Wall Street bankers, the "oil trust," the public utility interests. One of his favorite targets was Arkansas's senator Joe T. Robinson. Robinson was a senior member of the Little Rock law firm of Robinson, House, and Moses. In May, Long revealed the firm's client list, which included several big power companies in Arkansas and neighboring states. Huey had the list entered into the *Congressional Record*.[25]

Brough's reaction to the news that Huey Long was going to come to Arkansas and campaign for Mrs. Caraway was sarcastic; he said he could not ". . . help admire a man, who can make himself governor, senator, attorney general, and highway commissioner at the same time." He predicted the "Kingfish" would have his hands full when he started a fight in Arkansas. Brough and his supporters evidently did not think Senator Caraway presented a real challenge, even with Huey Long campaigning for her. One Brough admirer wrote Benton Kitchens:

> I'm wondering from whom Mrs. Caraway will take votes. I am sure that she will hurt Bodenhamer and take some from Miles, but I can not figure out where she will hurt Governor Brough.[26]

Prof. T. Harry Williams, in his biography of Huey Long, gives a vivid account of his crusade to re-elect Mrs. Caraway. In a chapter entitled "A Circus Hitched to a Tornado," Williams describes the superbly organized and efficient campaign, featuring sound trucks, distribution of huge amounts of campaign literature, and populistic messages by the Louisiana "Kingfish." In seven days he traveled over two thousand miles and gave about forty speeches, addressing a total of about two hundred thousand people. Mrs. Caraway accompanied him, of course, and gave speeches. But Long was in the spotlight, haranguing the crowds about the contrast between their economic condition and that of the greedy rich classes. Making a pitch for his plan for limiting incomes to a million dollars a year, he stirred their resentment with sarcastic remarks about the hardships this would impose on bankers and corporate executives. He praised Mrs. Caraway for her sensitivity to the problems of the common people and her courage in voting contrary to the Wall Street interests. He called on Arkansas voters to support this "brave little woman" against the "big men politicians."[27]

Brough seems to have been the only one of the six "big men politicians" who took public notice of Long's entrance into the campaign. His initial criticism of this meddling in Arkansas politics was mild; but he became more bitter after Long, speaking to twenty thousand at Little Rock, implied that Brough had supported efforts to impeach Long when the latter was governor of Louisiana. Brough denied the charge and asserted that Arkansas citizens did not need the advice of a "blustering egotistical demagogue." Political advertisements for Brough in the last days of the campaign assured voters that "'The Medicine Man' and His Sound Truck Ballyhoo" would not prevent a "rousing victory" for Brough; one ad asserted that, instead, Long's intervention was actually driving votes to Brough (presumably because of his speaking out against the "Kingfish"). The same ad contained a bold proclamation that "THE VICTORY IS WON" and urged voters to make it an overwhelming one. The Bodenhamer forces were likewise optimistic, announcing that reports from around the state indicated the El Dorado businessman would win by at least twenty thousand votes. Meanwhile, the Caraway campaign apparently used little if any newspaper advertising, although the Long-Caraway whirlwind speaking tour received plenty of press coverage—with the main focus on Huey's speeches. Thousands of pro-Caraway fliers were distributed by the campaign caravan. A pro-Brough citizen reported from Prescott: "'Hooey' put on his show at Prescott . . . and they flooded this county with literature in the interest of Mrs. Caraway." He added that he was unsure about how the electorate would be affected by Long's visit, but found it hard to believe that many of the people would follow such questionable leadership as exemplified by the Louisiana senator.[28]

This was wishful thinking, decisively refuted by Mrs. Caraway's resounding triumph on August 9. She received 128,000 votes, more than the combined total for Bodenhamer, Miles, and Brough. Considering the supreme confidence of Brough and followers, his fourth-place finish (with 26,656 votes) was rather humiliating. An *Arkansas Gazette* editorial described Mrs. Caraway's victory as "the most remarkable event in the history of Arkansas politics." The *Gazette* and other interpreters of the election agreed that Long's intervention was the decisive factor in her success; he was the "man of the hour," and his message aroused thousands who had known years of depression, unemployment, and low prices for farm products. However, analyses of the election—contemporary and later—pointed out that even before Long's invasion on her behalf, Mrs. Caraway had a great deal more political strength than her adversaries realized. Many distressed citizens, especially the small farmers, remembered Thaddeus Caraway as a champion of the ordinary people, and knew also that his widow's performance in the Senate so far indicated she was in the same tradition. Moreover, she probably received a greater share of the women's vote than any of her opponents—an ironic turn of events for Brough, who as governor had been a staunch advocate of women's suffrage. Still she could not have won without Huey Long.[29]

Brough and his followers were convinced that their campaign suffered most at the hands of the Kingfish, and that Brough would have won if Long had not meddled. Understandably bitter, Brough, in a letter to a friend, called Long a "tinpot Napoleon" who had spent $400,000 on the campaign for Mrs. Caraway. There are few, if any, additional records of the defeated candidate's reaction to the election; but a number of letters to Brough from supporters reveal the degree of shock and devastation they felt. Following are excerpts from seven such letters:

> We had the race won up to the entry of Kingfish in the campaign.

> Surely our people were swept off their feet and cast their ballot before they thought.

> I can think of no more perfect demonstration of complete ingratitude than the Voters of Arkansas have shown in their failure to send you to the Senate.

> If the "Kingfish" Long had remained in his own state, I believe you would have sweeped [sic] the State.

> I feel almost ashamed to live in a state that seems to prefer ballyhoo to brains.

> I am greatly hurt . . . that the election has turned to one so far less qualified to represent Arkansas in the United States Senate than you are.[30]

Along with lamentations, loyal friends offered consolation and assurances, such as the following remarks from a Conway salesman:

> While you feel the disappointment keenly, yet a man with your force of character and keen intellect will come to his own. You have been one of Arkansas' most useful citizens, both in public and private life. . . .[31]

Some students of Brough's 1932 campaign have concluded that the former governor probably would not have won, even if Huey Long had declined to help Mrs. Caraway. Reasons adduced for this assessment include the following: (1) Brough's excessive attention to such issues as bimetallism and tariff reduction had little appeal to Arkansas citizens, especially the distressed farmers; (2) the charge that he was backed by special interests, while unfair and unfounded, was significantly damaging to his cause; (3) many voters were alienated by Brough's support of Al Smith in 1928 and by his stand on the antievolution bill that same year; and (4) he was perceived as being in poor health, both mentally and physically, and too old to serve in public office.

With respect to the first argument it should be pointed out that *all* of the male candidates failed to arouse the voters as did Huey Long. It is doubtful that Brough "missed the mark" any further than the other five men, in articulating issues that the masses regarded as relevant to their economic condition. The claim that Brough was the "power trust" candidate was groundless, as evidenced by his austere campaign. The baselessness of the charge did not, however, prevent it from being accepted by some people (a Morrilton editor, for example); how widespread and damaging it was cannot be determined. Again, it is difficult to separate this consideration from Long's involvement in the race, for the Kingfish claimed that Brough, Miles, and perhaps all of Mrs. Caraway's opponents were somehow allied with "special interests" wishing to defeat the "little woman." As for the 1928 controversies, it is likely that Brough's loss of support among the "drys" and antievolutionists was offset by the admiration and respect many Arkansans accorded him for his courage in refusing to be "muzzled." Finally, regarding Brough's physical and mental condition, it is true that he did falter and become incoherent at one or two speaking engagements; on the whole, however, he seems to have demonstrated ample strength and stamina in a strenuous campaign that included several weeks of miserably hot weather. His ability to travel thousands of miles from March until August, delivering hundreds of speeches and addressing thousands of people, makes it difficult to put much credence in the assertion that he was old and infirm. Even in the aftermath of the automobile accident on July 4, the candidate canceled only a few engagements; he was on the campaign trail again on July 5. Moreover, only weeks after his defeat he possessed sufficient strength and character to embark upon a speechmaking tour on behalf of the Roosevelt-Garner ticket. As always a willing workhorse for the Democratic party, he made a tour of Kansas and Missouri, delivering a total of fifty-six speeches.[32]

Thus it seems that Brough, Bodenhamer, and Miles all had a chance to win the nomination—until Long intervened. It is impossible to determine which of these lost the most votes as a result of the Long-Caraway "blitz" during the final week. Perhaps it was Brough, since he was the only one who attacked Long, and thus by implication also attacked Mrs. Caraway. Such a lapse in chivalry was not intended by Brough. More characteristic of the scholar-gentleman was his congratulatory letter to her upon her victory in the November election. After praising her late husband for his "inestimable services to the nation," Brough expressed best wishes to the lady senator and closed the letter in his customary spirit of hospitality and good will:

> Mrs. Brough joins me in kindest personal regards and every wish for your success, and we both extend to you a very cordial invitation to be our guest, with your splendid sons, whenever you have occasion to visit Little Rock.[33]

CHAPTER 9

The Last Years

*B*ROUGH WAS CONSISTENT in his friendship and respect for Mrs. Caraway, choosing to focus his anger and bitterness upon Huey Long, whom he blamed for his defeat in the Senate primary. Two months after the election Brough asserted that he would have won by a plurality of thirty-five thousand votes had it not been for the Kingfish and his "lavish expenditure of money and distribution of liquor." During the succeeding years the Arkansan's opinion of the Kingfish dropped even lower, if possible, as the latter persisted in attacking Brough's idol, President Roosevelt, for not taking a more radical approach to the economic crisis. Brough customarily mellowed in his attitude toward adversaries, but apparently he could never find any redeeming virtues in the Louisiana senator. Commenting in a letter about the assassination of Long in September 1935, Brough lamented the manner of the senator's demise but appeared more relieved than saddened:

> the tragic end of his tempestuous career has removed one of the greatest menaces to President Roosevelt and Senator Robinson.[1]

Judging from Dr. Brough's correspondence he did not spend a great deal of time lamenting his rejection at the polls in August 1932; three days after the election he accepted an invitation to address the National Council of Teachers of English at Memphis in late November. His suggested topic was "Folklore of Arkansas," and he proposed to base his presentation on Fred W. Allsopp's *Folklore of Romantic Arkansas.* He was enthusiastic about books and in the last years of his life continued to read widely and add to his library, which consisted of several thousand volumes. He was especially interested in books about Arkansas and the South and was duly appreciative of the historical writings of George Fort Milton (on Stephen A. Douglas) and Douglas Southall Freeman (on George Washington). His delight in the works of Arkansas writers and editors such as Allsopp was closely linked with another of his interests—defending the state periodically against its detractors. (See chapter 6 for his spirited response to the *Vanity Fair* article by Travis Oliver.) Perhaps Brough's diverse interests, along with opportunities to travel and make speeches, were a key factor in the way he reacted to what might have been a crushing political setback.[2]

Meanwhile, Brough had joined the sales staff of the Mutual Life Insurance Company of New York; he claimed to be "very happy" in this work and expected to succeed at it. Little evidence remains regarding his career as an insurance salesman; however, there is reason to suspect that despite his many "contacts" and a definite salesmanship ability, he was not particularly successful. Although the state manager for Mutual, J. T. Thompson, recalled that Brough actually tried to memorize the rate tables, another contemporary believed that the former governor never really tried to sell insurance. Nevertheless, he had plenty of interests to occupy his attention, including numerous speaking engagements.[3]

With a national election at hand Brough was soon "on the circuit" making speeches on behalf of the Democratic Party, as he had often done before. Responding to an invitation from leading Democrats in Missouri and Kansas, Brough embarked upon a three-week speaking tour of those states, delivering fifty-six addresses for the Roosevelt-Garner national ticket and for local Democratic candidates. Representative of his partisan oratory was a speech he delivered in Kansas City and several other cities and towns in mid-October. Brough said the Democratic campaign was aimed at liberating the country from

> the tragic folly of the past four years during which we have experienced an orgy of speculation, a fiasco of governmental inefficiency, and a crash in the business structure . . . which beggars description.

He injected a bit of humor regarding President Hoover's promise to have the American people "on their feet" before the end of winter: "That certainly sounds discouraging. It was bad enough to have had them on their feet all summer. . . ." He blasted the Hoover and Coolidge administrations for policies favorable to the forces of "vested rights and predatory privilege," and lauded the prospect of a "new deal" under the leadership of Franklin D. Roosevelt.[4]

Soon after the November elections Brough received a letter from a high-ranking Kansas Democrat thanking him for his fine contribution to the Democratic success in most of the races. The letter also indicated Brough would have to wait a while for his expense check from the state committee, as the latter was "in the red." Other letters indicated Brough was an effective campaign speaker for the party in the two states. Whether he ever received the expense check from the party organization of either state is not known.[5]

As he had often done before, Brough wrote letters of congratulation to victorious Democratic candidates, including Roosevelt and Garner. In his letter to the president-elect, he expressed gratification at the latter's landslide triumph, and added the following laudatory comments on Roosevelt's final address on the eve of the election, calling it

> one of the most exquisite pieces of English I have ever heard. In the beauty and chasteness of its diction, in the sincerity of its emotions, and in the deep-seated humanity and dependence upon Almighty God which you voiced, it will rank as one of the classics of American eloquence.

Brough also mentioned having had the honor to campaign in Missouri and Kansas and indicated his gratification at the party's success in those states—especially Kansas, traditionally a Republican stronghold. Roosevelt wrote Brough expressing thanks for the congratulations, the praise of the final campaign speech, and the fruitful labor on the campaign trail.[6]

In view of the fact that Brough desired, and eventually received, a federal appointment in the Roosevelt administration, one may regard his flattering letters to Roosevelt, Garner, and other highly positioned Democrats such as Senator Robinson as a not-too-subtle attempt to ingratiate himself with those who might reward him for his yeoman service to the party. He had recently experienced a deeply disappointing rejection by the Arkansas voters and would not likely get another chance at a major elective office; yet politics and government were among his foremost interests. Moreover, his financial circumstances were apparently uncertain (although, as noted previously, little evidence remains concerning his insurance sales). Thus it is not surprising that he was eager to obtain a government position.[7]

However, Brough's propensity to flatter and congratulate, evident in hundreds of letters and speeches throughout his adult life, suggests that he would have penned the same sort of laudatory letters to victorious Democrats in 1932, whether or not he was seeking a political favor.

The political favor was long in coming; it was not received until March 1934. In the meantime, Brough asked friends to write in support of his quest for a federal post. In February 1933 C. M. Hirst of the Arkansas Department of Education wrote to Senator Robinson, urging him to present Brough's name to President Roosevelt for appointment to the Tariff Commission "or some other important Federal position." Hirst had studied under Brough at the University of Arkansas and had been impressed by the professor's lectures on tariff and reciprocity, which demonstrated a "thoroughgoing knowledge" of the subject. Brough seems to have avoided asking Robinson directly to use his influence with the president. One of Brough's letter writers, a judge from DeWitt, wrote Brough and quoted part of a "strong letter" from Senator Robinson. Robinson called Brough one of Arkansas's outstanding men and promised to do whatever he could for him. The judge then admonished the World War I governor to adopt the old Puritan maxim, "Why don't you speak for yourself." A few days later Robinson's willingness to help his long-time friend and loyal ally was reiterated in a letter to the Arkansas bank commissioner.[8]

Between the summer of 1933 and his eventual appointment to a newly created commission, Brough, optimistic as always, believed his elevation to some position in the government was imminent. In August Robinson assured him that the appointment was on the president's desk; early in January Brough expected to go to Washington "in the near future." A letter from Little Rock attorney J. S. Utley to President Roosevelt in early February reveals that Brough was being considered for a position on the Board of Railway Mediation. Naturally, Utley, whose friendship and political support stretched back some twenty-five years, gave Brough a hearty endorsement.[9]

When the long-awaited federal job was finally obtained, it was not a position on the Tariff Commission or the Railway Mediation Board, but the chairmanship of a special commission to settle a century-old boundary controversy between the District of Columbia and Virginia. In 1846 an act of Congress had given back to Virginia about ten square miles which the state had given to the district in the 1790s; however, the retrocession law did not satisfactorily define the boundary line. In 1934 Congress passed a measure providing for the appointment of a three-member commission to establish the boundary. The president was asked to appoint one member to represent the district, and a second member would be named by the state of Virginia; these two appointees would choose the third commissioner. The commission, which was given ten thousand dollars for its work, was to complete its report no later than March 1, 1935, and submit it to both Congress and the Virginia legislature. Commissioners were to be paid fifteen dollars per day, plus travel and subsistence expenses, and were authorized to hire assistants.[10]

Upon learning that President Roosevelt had selected him to represent the district, Brough, who was in the Washington area on a speaking engagement, telegraphed the good news to Anne in Little Rock and urged her to join him in Washington as soon as convenient. (The telegram states his pay as twenty dollars per day, evidently a mistake.) Anne drove to the capital, where she and her husband took up residence at the Kenesaw Apartments. They remained there until his death in December 1935.[11]

The Boundary Commission got off to a slow start; not until May did the Virginia governor appoint a representative for his state—William C. Gloth of Arlington. Brough and Gloth undertook a preliminary study of the boundary problem and selected the third commissioner, Malcolm S. McConihe of Washington. Brough served as chairman, although it is not clear whether this status was by virtue of his presidential appointment or by the vote of his two colleagues. In several letters written in 1934 Brough discussed the commission's work. It was "strenuous," but "very interesting and technical." Their deliberations concerned Supreme Court decisions, old land grants, charters, and compacts. They were dealing, he said, with $265 million worth of disputed land along the Potomac. He anticipated that Congress would probably extend the work of the commission.[12]

By early 1935 with the March 1 deadline approaching, Brough and his colleagues had heard some twenty-seven lawyers and considered "voluminous and technical" testimony. As Brough had predicted, Congress renewed the commission for another year and appropriated another ten thousand dollars. At the close of the hearings the commissioners prepared their report—which included thirty-two hundred pages of testimony—and submitted it both to Congress and to the Virginia legislature. As chairman, it was Brough's responsibility to defend the report before Congress, but he died a few days before his scheduled appearance. The commission's work was approved by the Virginia legislature on March 2, 1936. It faced a more difficult hurdle in the committee system of Congress, although ultimately the essential features of the proposed settlement were accepted.[13]

On the whole, the Broughs led an enjoyable and busy life in the nation's capital, although Anne suffered a wrist bone fracture in 1934 and a brief period of illness the following year. They entertained guests, attended White House social functions, and visited many historic and scenic sites in the area. They owned a car—one with only seventeen hundred miles on the odometer when they began their residence at the Kenesaw Apartments. Anne often drove Hillman to fill speaking engagements in and around Washington, and was also at the wheel when they went sight-seeing, at times with local acquaintances or with guests from Arkansas. A letter from Fred W. Allsopp of Little Rock thanked the Broughs for their hospitality and expressed special appreciation to Anne for driving them around the capital.[14]

The Broughs enjoyed life in Washington but missed their friends back home. And their friends missed them as well. One wrote,

> It seems your absence from the state causes your multitude of friends to miss you and appreciate you even more.

Apparently Brough did not get back to Little Rock more than once before his death, but Anne visited her brother Granville and his family for a few weeks in 1934. Because of his protracted absence from Little Rock, the former governor found it necessary to resign from a fraternity known as the xv Club, an exclusive, little-known fraternity to which he had belonged since becoming governor in 1917. This club, formed in 1904, consisted of fifteen business and professional men in the Little Rock area, who met twice a month to dine and discuss selected topics of political or cultural interest to the group. In his letter of resignation, Brough wrote:

> There is nothing . . . not even the Governorship of Arkansas, which I have more highly prized than my membership with [this] group of gentlemen, all of whom are gentlemen of wide, varied and accurate information.[15]

Through the newspapers and correspondence he kept up with Arkansas developments, as well as keeping the folks back home informed of his Washington activities. Letters and newspaper clippings in the scrapbooks indicate he was actively interested in the Arkansas centennial celebration being planned for 1936, the state parks, and the Little Rock Civic Music Association.[16]

Brough's letters abound with good will, friendliness, and a genuine interest in the recipient's health, work, achievements, sorrows, et cetera. Typical of his expressions of sympathy are his consoling words to a Conway friend upon the death of his mother. "Her life and her memory will be a benediction through the years to her splendid children of six sons and one daughter." In his customary hospitable way he invited the bereaved friend to come visit them in Washington, assuring him that "the latch-string will always be on the outside of our hearts and homes for you and yours. . . ." The Broughs were sincere in wanting visitors—especially from Arkansas. They urged them to come to Washington and plan on staying with them, for they had a studio couch in the apartment which could be converted into a bed for guests. In trying to encourage one Arkansas friend to come to the capital, he emphasized the availability of inexpensive meals in the cafeteria in their apartment building—twenty-five cents for a wholesome breakfast, sixty-five cents for a complete dinner.[17]

Despite the arduousness of his Boundary Commission work, Brough delivered a large number of speeches in 1934 and 1935; his speaking schedule was reminiscent of his peak years on the chautauqua circuits. At one point in 1934 he was averaging two or three speeches a week, and the pace increased somewhat the next year. Often his topics were the same ones he had expounded on since his earliest oratorical forays, and at times he worked into his address some sort of defense of, or boost for, Arkansas. For example, he told an architects' club about Arkansas's success in growing cotton and rice and about its various mineral resources, such as bauxite. He also bragged that in the mountain counties of the state could be found "the purest strain of Anglo-Saxon blood of this Continent." Following are some examples of his speaking engagements in 1934 and 1935. While incomplete, the list reflects the varied and busy speaking schedule he followed:

> Manassas, Virginia battlefield
> July 4 oration at Washington Monument (1934)
> Mississippi Federation of Women's Clubs (Jackson)
> Series of political speeches in several midwestern states
> Jackson Day dinner
> Democratic League, District of Columbia
> Cumberland (Md.) Rotary
> Gettysburg (Pa.) Rotary
> Adults Bible Class Francis Asbury M. E. Church
> Baltimore Lions Club
> Nationwide radio address on the Park System[18]

The highlight of all this speechmaking was his ten-minute patriotic oration given as part of the capital's July 4 celebration in 1934. Brough was selected as the only speaker for the evening program, an hour-long affair which was presented before a crowd of about one hundred thousand gathered around the Washington monument. The program was broadcast, although the extent of the radio audience is not known. Back in Little Rock, Brough's long-time friend and supporter J. S. Utley promised to tune in, noting that selection of Dr. Brough for the occasion would "give Arkansas some prominence that it could not get in any other way." In addition to Brough's short speech the enthusiastic crowd was treated to music by the army band, a reading of the Declaration of Independence, and an elaborate fireworks display.[19]

Prior to the program a police escort cleared the streets for "the Governor and his party," which included the Broughs and about thirty other Arkansans. In his address, Brough paid high tribute to President and Mrs. Roosevelt, and to Senate majority leader Joe T. Robinson. He pointed out that the president and his wife were descended from prominent Americans of the colonial and revolutionary era. He also denounced Hitler for his persecution of the Jews.

According to a Pennsylvania congressman (a former Arkansan), Brough was interrupted several times by the tumultuous crowd.[20]

Brough died of a heart attack on the morning after Christmas, 1935, in their apartment in Washington. Upon his request, Mrs. Brough went to bring him a newspaper; when she returned he was dead. Although he had been ill for a few days, he apparently had begun to feel better with the arrival of the holiday. In fact, only a short time before his death he had remarked to his wife on the "beautiful Christmas" they had enjoyed. One of the many eulogies evoked by Brough's passing suggested that these "last words" were appropriate for a man who "loved doing . . . beautiful, kindly things":

> Christmas gave his nature a fine occasion for the beautiful expressions of kindness and generosity.[21]

There were many such tributes—from Senators Robinson and Caraway, the governor and other state officials, former students and colleagues in education, numerous friends and supporters, including some from his gubernatorial years. A former student, in a letter published in the *Memphis Commercial Appeal,* called Dr. Brough "an inspirational teacher," "Arkansas' ambassador of good will," and "one of America's finest examples of the scholar in politics." Some of the letters of sympathy to Anne Brough were from educators: A. M. Harding, director of the University of Arkansas Extension Service, noted that ". . . the school men of the state [had] always looked upon Dr. Brough as the Educational Governor of Arkansas," and the president of Arkansas State University wrote of the ". . . debt of gratitude for his vision and service in the interest of the education of the youth of this state."[22]

Brief services were held in Washington on the day of Brough's death. Then the body was brought to Little Rock, arriving on Saturday, December 28, and taken to the family home on Arch Street, where hundreds of friends called. With Mrs. Brough's approval, Gov. Marion Futrell arranged to honor Charles Hillman Brough with a full state funeral. He ordered that flags over public buildings be flown at half-mast on Saturday and Sunday. At 10 A.M. on Sunday a guard of honor from the Arkansas National Guard accompanied the body from the family home to the capitol and remained beside it in the rotunda as large numbers of mourners filed past the casket. Shortly after noon, the guardsmen then formed a procession which escorted the funeral hearse to the Second Baptist Church on Scott Street, where services were conducted by Rev. Calvin Waller, who had been the Broughs' pastor since around 1917. Among those attending the services were Senator Robinson, Rep. D. D. Terry, Governor Futrell, the justices of the Arkansas Supreme Court, and four former governors. In his sermon the Reverend Mr. Waller described Brough as "a scholar, statesman, philanthropist, orator and Christian gentleman. . . ." He was ". . . loyal to his friends and family, true to his country and flag, and devoted to the cause of the Lord." The *Arkansas Gazette* obituary noted that the church auditorium was filled with citizens from all around the state, despite the icy conditions resulting from sleet and snow. Following the funeral Dr. Brough was buried at Roselawn Cemetery.[23]

Epilogue

Certain aspects of Brough's personality and character are clearly discernible in his correspondence, and in the recollections of family members, friends, and acquaintances. These sources depict an affable, considerate, and accommodating person whose manners and morals were essentially shaped by the southern and Baptist environment into which he was born and in which he spent most of his youth. As noted in chapter 1, the predominant adult influences on Brough as a youngster were Uncle Walter and Aunt Adelia Hillman, who assumed care over him (and his brother) at an early age.

We may assume that the boys' mother, who taught at the Female Institute, shared the moral and religious ideals of the Hillmans. In any case, Flora Brough's short span of motherhood, although it may have been formative, is one of obscurity insofar as the extant records are concerned. As for the influence of Brough's father on the son's personality and character, the available evidence provides nothing to indicate the extent of such influence during the pre-college period. Almost all of the materials pertaining to father-son relations concern Charles Hillman's college years—for example, the letter he wrote to his father describing his success on the Ph.D. examinations at Johns Hopkins. This letter and other sources clearly express filial love and respect. The young scholar also valued his father's advice; for example, when *Irrigation in Utah* was not selling well, the elder Brough imparted to his son the old adage, "If you want to have a thing done well, do it yourself." Seizing upon those words of wisdom, the author got busy and sold an impressive number of copies, mostly to Mormon families in the Ogden area.[1]

Still, it appears clear that parental influences were overshadowed by those of his uncle and aunt. In fact, Dr. Brough, reflecting years later on his pleasant childhood, specifically credited the Hillmans for preparing him for life. In addition to their moral and spiritual example and instruction, Brough fondly recalled such childhood activities as picking cotton for Uncle Walter (who owned seven plantations) and catching rats and other vermin that infested the plantation storehouses. Another experience from those Clinton years had specific relevance to his future career as a public speaker; as told by Mrs. Fay Williams, in her *Arkansans of the Years,* young Brough (age twelve) delivered a speech on "dirt daubers," based in large part on his collection of over twenty-five hundred dirt-dauber nests! The occasion, and the audience, for this oratorical effort are not known.

As noted in the opening chapter, one interpreter of Brough theorizes that the separation from his parents at an early age may have produced in the son a sense of insecurity. Particular emphasis is given to separation from his father, who remained in Utah and left the boys at Clinton, even after the death of his wife. The theory suggests that the feeling of insecurity fostered in Hillman Brough an obsessive desire for approbation and confirmation of his worth; thus his tendency to flatter others (and perhaps seek flattery from them) and his tendency to overextend himself in pleasing others; for example, his often exhausting schedule of speaking engagements for both "large" and "small" occasions. These characteristics (vulnerability to flattery and willingness to overextend himself) have also been discerned by a Little Rock psychologist, from a recent analysis of Brough's handwriting.[2]

Insufficient evidence obliges us to be cautious regarding parental impressions on Charles Hillman Brough. We can more profitably enlarge our understanding of him by looking further at the long-term impact of the Clinton environment and at the moral and spiritual guidance provided by the Hillmans. Because of these influences he maintained a life-long, and very active, connection with the Southern Baptist Church. This attachment was evidenced in his numerous church-related activities as a young professor at Clinton and later at Fayetteville: lecturing at religious gatherings, teaching a young women's Sunday School class, serving as a church deacon, "filling pulpits" as a lay speaker, and promoting the work of the YMCA. (The time and energy thus devoted illustrate one of the maxims which both he and his father liked to quote in evaluating the achievements of others: "great, in the arduous greatness of things done.") Throughout his life Brough was highly esteemed by ministers and leading laymen in the Baptist and other churches, and their cordiality and respect were reciprocated by him. It is true that while president of Central Baptist College in Conway, Brough became embroiled in a feud with conservative Baptists over politics and evolution. But many church members were on Brough's side in this squabble, and over the years church leaders held Brough in high regard as a Christian gentleman. One of his pastors from the Fayetteville period, writing in 1941, paid tribute to his "bigness of heart and loyalty to his pastor" and described him as one of the most loyal deacons he had ever had; some years later a book on the history of Arkansas Baptists highlighted Brough's contributions to the church.[3]

Brough's extensive education, wide reading, and travels led him away from narrow dogmatism to a broader, more tolerant outlook. And yet, except for the controversies of 1928–29, he managed to maintain a comfortable rapport with the conservative as well as moderate members of the denomination.

On the matter of white-black relations Brough remained conservative, regarding black people as inferior and supporting both segregation and disfranchisment. These views were evident in the young professor's article on the Clinton riot of 1874. Since he grew up in Clinton, it is not surprising that he vilified the "carpetbagger" government of Adelbert Ames. Brough's racism was later tempered by a paternalistic outlook, which characterized many southern progressives involved in the "social uplift" efforts of the Southern Sociological Congress. Paternalism was consistent with maintaining white supremacy, and in 1916 candidate Brough and his campaign advisers made a great effort to prove he was "safe" on the race question. As governor he seemed sincerely to desire an improvement in race relations; yet, when the rioting in Phillips County broke out he almost instinctively identified with the white leaders there and readily accepted their explanation of the troubles.

Having reviewed the early influences on Brough's character and personality, let us turn now to his ability to "win friends and influence people"— which served him well as a political candidate in 1916 and 1918 (but obviously had declined by the senatorial race of 1932). One reason he attracted friends and loyal supporters was his constant demonstration that he was interested in other people, their aspirations, their problems, et cetera. His replies to letters usually were characterized by a careful specificity; rarely do they cause the recipient to feel that the writer was too busy to do more than "dash off" a quick response. His remarkable memory no doubt facilitated the writing or dictation of letters of this kind without expending much time looking up specific facts.

Many stories have been told of Brough's amazing memory. Fay Williams recounts the following one in *Arkansans of the Years:*

> A man named T. L. Vaughn was introduced briefly to Dr. Brough on the street in front of a hotel. They were both in a hurry, and had no time for conversation. Some weeks later, as Vaughn was making his way through a crowded downtown area, Brough spotted him in the crowd and said, "How do you do, Mr. T. L. Vaughn?" Astonished, Vaughn said, "Wait a minute, you only met me once." Brough said yes, then told Vaughn the time and place of their earlier brief encounter.

Karr Shannon, a Little Rock journalist, wrote about Brough's memory skills in a 1960 feature article in the *Arkansas Democrat.* Shannon first met Brough in 1930 when the latter came to Melbourne, Arkansas, to deliver a speech at the Izard County Teachers' Institute. Shannon was county superintendent of schools and Brough was a special lecturer for the University of Arkansas Extension Service. Shannon met Brough at the train depot in Batesville and drove him to Melbourne, where he was to speak to the teachers at the courthouse. During the thirty-mile automobile trip, Brough read a newspaper, smoked cigarettes, and "grilled" his driver about Izard County—asking numeous questions about its history, officials, leading citizens, and so forth. Shannon answered many of Brough's questions, and in addition handed him a copy of a history of Izard County (which Shannon had written). Brough quickly read the 127-page book. Later, before a capacity crowd at the courthouse, he began his speech with "information and eulogies" on the county, rolling off names, dates, events which he had learned only a short time before, as he was being driven to Melbourne. It was a well-organized and accurate introduction; he did not err on any name, date, or event. "To this day," wrote Shannon, "people in Izard County marvel at his [Brough's] vast knowledge of their county."[4]

This ability to demonstrate his interest in and knowledge of people—whether he was addressing an audience, writing a letter, or remembering individuals' names—was an important key to Brough's popularity. In his speechmaking he often recognized, and called the names of, persons sitting near the platform; he would sometimes tell jokes on them or perhaps use some fact about them to illustrate a point. Moreover, whether on or off the platform he did not allow his scholarly interests, erudition, and wide reading to produce an image of an "egghead"; instead he managed to remain "simple and human in all his inclinations." Members of organizations which Brough addressed frequently remarked upon his pleasant personality as well as his speaking ability. He was a good "mixer," even when not running for office, and when on a train would typically walk through the cars, introducing himself, shaking hands, and making friends. He was an excellent raconteur and enjoyed playing checkers and contract bridge.[5]

Thus, with reference to "Brough the man," the biographer finds himself in somewhat the position of a eulogist, presenting a most positive evaluation of an honoree at a testimonial dinner. There is a temptation simply to seize upon clichés like "a scholar and a gentleman," who harbored "malice toward none."

The records do not reveal acts of corruption or chicanery while he was governor; in fact, he was rare in that he was in worse financial condition when he left office than when he entered it. As for marital discord or other strained family relations, surely these occurred to some degree, but without evidence we cannot assert this as true. Ever the sentimentalist, Brough delighted in the

Christmas holidays; his correspondence includes many letters to family members and friends, thanking them for cards or gifts or telling them he is sending a present. Harry L. Ponder of Walnut Ridge, whose father served in the state senate while Brough was governor, recalls that he and his brothers and sisters received a book from Brough each Christmas for a number of years. Brough was also dutiful to remember his wife ("Miss Anne") on such occasions as Valentine's Day and their wedding anniversary.[6]

The author of a master's thesis summarized "Brough the man" as follows:

> The picture is of a sensitive, learned man—one not profoundly original in his thinking. This man was intensely anxious to please, to use his education and experience in aiding mankind, to bring his fellows pleasure and diversion, and to scatter the glories of his beloved and adopted state . . . along the chautauqua trail.[7]

His life story certainly is devoid of those salacious elements which characterize many modern biographies; however, it is far from a dull one for those who can see in it the personification of many interesting and important segments of Arkansas and southern history, cultural and social as well as political.

Appendix

Excerpts from Selected Speeches by Charles Hillman Brough

The following excerpts illustrate several kinds of addresses by Dr. Brough—commemorative, political, patriotic, "boost Arkansas," and chautauqua/lyceum.

To the Daughters of the Confederacy,
Fayetteville, January 1907

To-day, dowered with hearts of reverence and kindling the sacred fires of patriotism on the altar of our every heart, this pilgrimmage [sic] of southern manhood and southern womanhood on the one hundredth anniversary of the birth of our illustrious chieftain, Robert Edward Lee, is journeying in silence to his tomb to lay offerings of honor and love on the shrine of Dixie's greatest defender.

And this, indeed, is a glorious custom and perhaps a matchless privilege, for standing in our imagination beside the grave of Lee whose very earth has drunk in the communion wine of southern valor and whose coverlid of Nature's green has been watered by a patriot's blood, methinks that the sons and daughters of proud cavaliers will press to their lips this cup of sorrow filled by the tears of the widows and fatherless and toast the Stars and Bars which still in sweet remembrance wave, O'er the homes of the free and the hearts of the brave. Nay, even more, impelled by the glorious inspiration of Lee's matchless life and character, I doubt not, my friends, that every one who catches the echoing strains of martial music and sees in his imagination the march of tattered and dust stained veterans o'er old Virginia's hills feels prouder than ever before that he wears the badge of southern ancestry; that he will believe that each of the eleven stars emblemmatic [sic] of a State that twinkled in the firmament of the Stars and Bars irradiated the light of liberty and local self-government. . . .

Campaign for Governor (Democratic Primary), Russellville, November 1915

In presenting my name to the voters of the State of Arkansas for the highest office within their gift, that of Governor, I do so with the deep realization of the responsibility and labor attached to the work of the Executive. However, believing that the time is ripe in our commonwealth for a clean, progressive administration of its affairs, free from the rancor and turmoil of personal political strife, I enter this race with the determination to consecrate all the ability and character I possess to the moral, educational, and financial betterment of the State.

At the outset, let it be understood I am the candidate of no faction or clique, the champion of no institution or vested interest, but my candidacy is predicated solely upon the belief that I can be an instrument in the hands of the people to redeem Arkansas from any charge of corrupt politics and machine rule . . .

If elected, I pledge the State of Arkansas a safe, sane, business administration; the Statehouse will not be a laboratory for experiment with political theories, but a practical workhouse with open doors, where all the people, rich and poor alike, will be welcomed for consultation with the Governor. I shall enter the office free from political entanglements, with a fixed determination to bring about a spirit of co-operation and eliminate factional strife, to the end that we may have an administration based on efficiency, political ideals characterized by purity, and a Democracy ennobled by achievement. . . .

To the Biennial Meeting of the Federation of Women's Clubs (Hot Springs, Arkansas), April 1918

. . . The state of Arkansas genuinely appreciates the honor of entertaining the Biennial meeting of the Federation of Women's Clubs of Arkansas as it is composed of some of the choicest representatives of women whose lives have been consecrated to the spirit of service. We recognize that the Federation is one of the most important agencies for good in our country, particularly so, in this hour of our Nation's greatest crisis. An organization having a membership of approximately 2,000,000 enrolled in 9,818 clubs, of which there are 213 clubs with 10,000 members in our own state, is calculated to do a mighty work in making the world safe for democracy and democracy safe for the world. . . .

In Arkansas seventy thousand women have registered for definite service in connection with the great war of liberty and democracy against German autocracy and despotism and, throughout the United States, the women are displaying the same fortitude, the same sacrifice and heroism that character- izes the four million noble women of England and the three million heroic women of France in manning the munition factories of our brave allies. . . .

We feel sure that the thousands of cultured and charming delegates who . . . will represent your organization will not only find your deliberations at Hot Springs profitable but that the curative waters and the scenic beauties of our famous health resort, will give you a new lease on life. After spending eight days at Hot Springs . . . you [will] visit Little Rock . . . the site of one of the six- teen cantonments of the United States Army, where from 35,000 to 40,000 sol- diers are in training to place their bodies as living walls between the cause of liberty and democracy and the Huns who would destroy them. . . .

To Visiting Delegation of Business Leaders from Kansas City, Assembled with the Little Rock Board of Commerce, Little Rock, April 1924

We are particularly delighted to be your hosts tonight, and that you should have honored us on your Deluxe tour of the southwest, because we realize that Arkansas, a land of unrivaled opportunity, has been cartooned and cari- catured more than any other State in the American Union. . . .

We are . . . delighted at the opportunity to present to you the opportunity to refute these slanders for yourselves, after a personal inspection of several of our cities, and a trip through a number of our smaller communities, evi- dencing culture, courage and progress on the part of our citizenship. We wel- come the opportunity of telling you that in 1923 our Wonder State produced the fifth largest cotton crop in the American Union . . . that our rice crop in 1923 of 7,500,000 bushels represented the third largest yield in our country . . . that, with an annual cut of approximately two billion board feet of lum- ber, we rank fourth among the States in our total cut of timber. . . .

With cheap and abundant power, a steady and reliable labor supply, 75% of whom are native white born Americans, a colored population that is law abiding and interested in the development of our City and State, this central market of normally a million bale cotton State, with a salubrious climate, averaging a rainfall of only 48 inches annually, a cultured, contented and God- fearing citizenship, welcomes this 33rd Trade Extension Trip of the Kansas City Chamber of Commerce. . . .

From a Representative Chautauqua Address, "America's Leadership of the World"

Barely more than three hundred years ago, amid solemn prayers from shore and sea, a frail yet sturdy bark hauled up its anchorage in the ports of princely power and, launched on untried billows, set sail in quest of freedom. There was no pilot at the wheel; the star that guided her was the undimmed constellation of civil and religious liberty. There was no captain in the stateroom; her deck was the altar of the living God. True it is how a tempestuous voyage unsettled the course of the mariner's compass, that the elements lashed their froth and fury against a mast and sail as yet untouched by the ocean's spray; but the fervent hymns of those patriotic Pilgrims, set to music on tattered shrouds and rigging, sung by America's sons and daughters the first anthem of a New World's independence. Thus, six generations have barely passed away since this unhailed and unwelcome Mayflower was our only ship of State and the frozen and neglected Rock of Plymouth was the harbor of our safety. But now, thanks to the God of freedom and the free, we can boast of a glorious Ship of State and a Union strong and great. "We know what Master laid thy keel, what Workman wrought thy ribs of steel, No lowering clouds or howling gales can rend thy sails, Thy Anchorage is the anchorage of a people's hope."

The American Constitution, the one hundred and thirty-seventh anniversary of the adoption of which we have just observed, was pronounced by William E. Gladstone, the "Grand Old Man of England," and on his recent tour of the United States by David Lloyd George, perhaps the most brilliant statesman today, as "the most wonderful work ever struck off at a given time by the brain and purpose of man." By virtue of its elastic provisions, men and women of all countries and all creeds have been brought together and inspired with a passionate loyalty; and, whether the material thrown into the crucible be the thoughtful Englishman, the jolly and eloquent Irishman, the honest Scotchman, the brilliant Frenchman, the hard-working and colorful Italian— whatever be his nationality—it emerges from the melting pot purged of most of its dross and shines forth as the purest ingot of humanity—the modern American. With little Holland, we present the first instance in organic history of the absolute separation of church and state and the fight of every man and woman to worship God according to the dictates of their own consciences; and we furnish the only instance in constitutional law, where there is a separation of powers between the executive, legislative, and judicial departments of government. . . .

Notes

Chapter 1

1. Frank L. Klement, *The Limits of Dissent: Clement L. Vallandigham and the Civil War* (Lexington: University of Kentucky Press, 1970), 64, 229.

2. Clipping from the *Los Angeles Times,* 20 November 1910, in Brough-Roark Scrapbooks, in the General Microfilm Files (7 rolls) at History Commission, Little Rock, Roll 1. Hereafter most references to this source will be cited as BRS plus the roll number. Charles Orson Cook, "Arkansas's Charles Hillman Brough: An Interpretation," (Ph.D. diss., University of Houston, 1980), 13; Central Female Institute, *Annual Catalogue, 1872–73;* U.S. Bureau of Census, *Tenth Census,* 1880; *Baptist Record* (Clinton, Miss.), 13 August 1885; Fay Williams, *Arkansans of the Years,* 4 vols. (Little Rock: Allard, 1951), I, 61–62; U.S. Bureau of Census, *Ninth Census,* 1870; Hinds County Marriage Records, on microfilm at Mississippi Department of Archives and History, Jackson, Roll 140; H. M. Weathersby, "Alumni Department," *Mississippi College Magazine* 10 (February 1904): 23; Dunbar Rowland, *History of Mississippi: The Heart of the South,* 4 vols. (Chicago-Jackson: S. J. Clarke Company, 1925), IV, 153.

3. *Tenth Census,* 1880; Weathersby, "Alumni Department," 23; *Baptist Record,* 13 August 1885.

4. *Ogden City Directory,* 1890, p. 10; 1892–93, p. 86; clipping from *Fayetteville Daily Democrat,* n.d., BRS, Roll 1; Richard C. Roberts and Richard W. Sadler, *Ogden: Junction City* (Northbridge, Calif., 1985), 35; *Ogden* (Utah) *Standard,* 9 November 1892 and 7 November 1893; U.S. Census Bureau, *Twelfth Census,* 1900.

5. L. S. Foster, *Mississippi Baptist Preachers* (St. Louis: National Baptist Publishing Company, 1895), 379–81.

6. *Biographical and Historical Memoirs of Mississippi,* 2 vols. (Chicago: Goodspeed Publishing Company, 1891), I, 933–34; Hillman College, *Sixty-Eighth Annual Catalogue,* 1922–23, p. 8.

7. *Biographical and Historical Memoirs of Mississippi,* I, 933; Walter Hillman, "A Plea for Common Schools," ten-page pamphlet in Mississippi Archives, n.p., n.d.; Foster, *Mississippi Baptist Preachers,* 381; "Central Female Institute," clipping from *Tri-Weekly Clarion,* 4 September 1869, in subject file, Mississippi Archives; *Biographical and Historical Memoirs of Mississippi,* I, 934; Mrs. Kitty A. Vaughn, typescript biographical sketch of Dr. Walter Hillman, in Mississippi Archives.

8. "Antebellum Hillman," two-page typescript, n.d., in Mississippi College Collection, Mississippi College, Clinton; *Baptist Record,* 13 and 14 August 1884; Central Female Institute, *Annual Catalogue,* 1872–73, p. 19.

9. "Report of Boyhood Days of Charles Hillman Brough," Little Rock, 11 October 1923, BRS, Roll 1.

10. Cook, "Arkansas's Charles Hillman Brough," 24; BRS, Roll 1.

11. Brough, "Historic Clinton," in *Publications of the Mississippi Historical Society* 7 (Oxford, Miss., 1902): 311.

12. Mississippi College, *Catalogue*, 1891–92 (Brandon, Miss.: E. B. Tabor, 1892), pp. 32–34.

13. Ibid., 15; Mississippi College, *Catalogue*, 1892–93, p. 12; invitation to 42nd Anniversary of Philomathean Society of Mississippi College, 28 April 1894; BRS, Roll 1; Mississippi College, *Catalogue*, 1893–94, p. 11.

14. Weathersby, "Alumni Department," 24; U.S. Census Bureau, *Twelfth Census*, 1900; *Ogden City Directory*, 1890–91, 1892–93, 1899; "Utah Historical Records Survey Project," in Special Collections Department of Utah University Library (mimeographed, 1940), 25; *Ogden* (Utah) *Standard*, 13, 14, and 28 October 1893, 8 November 1893; Milton R. Hunter, *Beneath Ben Lomond's Peak: A History of Weber County, 1824–1900* (Salt Lake City: Deseret News Press, 1944), 475.

15. *Ogden Standard*, 8 April 1894; 10 April 1894; 12 April 1894; 7 July 1894; 9 July 1894; 10 July 1894.

16. Ibid., 2 September 1896; 8 October 1893; 9 September 1896; 18 June 1896; 4 September 1896; 11 July 1896.

17. *Ogden City Directory*, 1895–96, p. 67; *Ogden Standard*, 30 August 1896.

18. *Ogden Standard*, 1 September 1896 and 4 September 1896.

19. BRS, Roll 1; Hugh Hawkins, *A History of the Johns Hopkins University, 1874–1889* (Ithaca: Cornell University Press, 1960), 173; John Spencer Bassett, "Herbert Baxter Adams," in *Dictionary of American Biography*, 20 volumes plus supplements, ed. Allen Johnson, Dumas Malone, et al. (New York: Charles Scribner's Sons, 1928–1958), I, 69–70; John Higham, *History: The Development of Historical Studies in the United States* (Englewood Cliffs, N.J.: Prentice-Hall, Inc., 1965), 11, 13; speech by Brough delivered 29 November 1915 at Russellville, in Charles Hillman Brough Papers, Special Collections Division of Mullins Library at the University of Arkansas, Fayetteville (hereafter cited as Brough Papers).

20. Weathersby, "Alumni Department," 24; clipping from *Ogden Standard*, 16 November 1897, in BRS, Roll 1; printed program for Johns Hopkins commencement exercises for 14 June 1898, in BRS, Roll 1; Cook, "Arkansas's Charles Hillman Brough," 18; clipping from *Washington* (D.C.) *Post*, 27 June 1898, BRS, Roll 1; C. L. Stevenson to Brough, 22 June 1898, Brough Papers; Williams, *Arkansans of the Years*, I, 62.

21. Charles Hillman Brough, *Irrigation in Utah* (Baltimore: Johns Hopkins University Press, 1898).

22. Charles Hillman Brough to Charles Milton Brough, 9 June 1898, BRS, Roll 1; telegram from Charles Milton Brough to Charles Hillman Brough, 13 June 1898, ibid.; Weathersby, "Alumni Department," 24.

Chapter 2

1. Copies of letters by Professors Sidney Sherwood and Herbert Baxter Adams (with concurrence of President Gilman), April 1898, Brough Papers; handwritten copies of letters by Frank J. Dawson and Frederick H. Newell, June 1897; clipping from *Ogden* (Utah) *Bimetallist,* 3 September 1898, in BRS, Roll 1.

2. Mississippi College, *Catalogue,* 1898–99, pp. 24–25; Mississippi College, *Annual Register,* 1901–02, p. 51; Mississippi College, *Catalogue,* 1900–01, p. 28.

3. Mississippi College, *Catalogue,* 1891–92, p. 28; *Catalogue,* 1898–99, pp. 24–27.

4. Herbert Baxter Adams, Baltimore, to Brough, 13 March 1899, Brough Papers; *Mississippi College Magazine* 7 (October 1900): 18.

5. Brochure in BRS, Roll 1; clippings from *The Baptist* (n.d.), and from the *Ogden Standard,* 20 May 1901, both in BRS, Roll 1; Ralph William Widener, "The Political Campaign Speaking of Charles Hillman Brough in 1916 and 1932" (Ph.D. diss., Southern Illinois University, 1962), 39; clipping from *Magnolia Gazette,* 9 August 1899, in BRS, Roll 1.

6. Jackson, *Mississippi Daily Herald,* 1 January 1900; *The Baptist,* 15 August 1901.

7. Hollander, Baltimore, to Brough, 25 January 1899 and 12 June 1899; Adams to Brough, 13 March 1899, Brough Papers.

8. *Mississippi College Magazine* 7 (March 1900): 4–15; 9 (October 1902): 3–17; *Publications of the Mississippi Historical Society,* ed. Franklin L. Riley, vols. 2, 6, and 7; Weathersby, "Alumni Department," 25.

9. Charles S. Sydnor, ed., "Letters from Franklin L. Riley to Herbert B. Adams, 1894–1901," *Journal of Mississippi History* 2 (January 1940): 101, 108; Weathersby, "Alumni Department," 24; BRS, Roll 1.

10. BRS, Roll 1; University of Mississippi, *Catalogue,* 1902–03, pp. 141–42; University of Mississippi, *Magazine* 25 (December 1901), 5–9; Franklin L. Riley, ed., "Proceedings of the Fifth Annual Meeting of the Mississippi Historical Society," *Publications of the Mississippi Historical Society* 6 (1902): 9–13, 53–63.

11. Riley, "Proceedings of the Fifth Annual Meeting of the Mississippi Historical Society," 53–63; James Wilford Garner, *Reconstruction in Mississippi* (Baton Rouge, La.: 1901), 378–79.

12. Riley, "To Whom It May Concern," 3 June 1902; Sydnor, "Letters," 100; Dunbar Rowland, *First Annual Report of the Director of the Department of Archives and History of the State of Mississippi* (Jackson, Miss., 1911), 6; Robert Reynolds Simpson, "The Origins of State Departments of Archives and History in the South" (Ph.D. diss., University of Mississippi, 1971), 139.

13. Riley, "To Whom It May Concern," 3 June 1902; G. D. Shands, University, Mississippi, "To Whom It May Concern," 31 May 1902; Frank J. Cannon, Salt Lake City, to Brough, 9 June 1902, Brough Papers.

14. Weathersby, "Alumni Department," 24–25; Widener, "The Political Campaign Speaking of Charles Hillman Brough in 1916 and 1932," 41; printed leaflet

titled "Hillman College," announcing new teachers for 1902–03, in Mississippi College Collection, Mississippi College Library.

15. Advertisement in *The Hillman Lesbidelian* 1 (May 1903): Mississippi College Collection; Federal Writers' Project, *Mississippi: A Guide to the Magnolia State* (New York: Hastings House, 1949), 311; Central Female Institute, *Annual Catalogue,* 1872–73, pp. 18–19, *The Hillman Lesbidelian* 3 (May 1906): 4, Mississippi College Collection.

16. Clipping from *Jackson Clarion-Ledger,* 26 November 1902, BRS, Roll 1; Rowland, *History of Mississippi,* IV, 153; A. M. Longine, "To Whom It May Concern," 3 March 1903; John L. Johnson, "To Whom It May Concern," 18 March 1903; Rev. W. T. Lowrey, "To Whom It May Concern," 19 March 1903; Henry L. Whitfield, "To Whom It May Concern," 27 April 1903, Brough Papers.

17. Weathersby, "Alumni Department," 25.

18. *History of the University of Arkansas,* a special centennial publication sponsored by the University of Arkansas Foundation (Little Rock: S. M. Brooks Agency, Inc., 1972), 3; Robert A. Leflar, *First Hundred Years: Centennial History of the University of Arkansas* (1972), 71–72; *University Newsletter,* 1 December 1903, BRS, Roll 1.

19. University of Arkansas, *Catalogue,* 1905–06, p. 96; 1907–09, p. 98; 1905–06, pp. 96–98.

20. Hollander to Brough, 15 October 1903, Brough Papers.

21. *University Newsletter,* 1 December 1903; Widener, "The Political Campaign Speaking of Charles Hillman Brough in 1916 and 1932," 41; *X-Ray* (a student newspaper), 11 March 1904; "A Southern Evening," program for benefit of University Athletic Association, 11 March 1904, BRS, Roll 1.

22. Author's interview with Mrs. Evadna Roark, Little Rock, 14 August 1987; *The Cardinal,* vol. 7 (1903–04), 191; vol. 8 (1904–05), 177; vol. 13 (1910), 17.

23. Widener, "The Political Campaign Speaking of Charles Hillman Brough in 1916 and 1932," 42.

24. Ibid., 43.

25. "A Southern Evening"; clipping from *Springdale Daily Leader,* 22 December 1911, Brough Papers; *Fayetteville Daily Democrat,* 19 January 1907.

26. *Fayetteville Daily Democrat,* 26 October 1909.

27. Charles Wann Crawford, "Charles Hillman Brough: Educator and Politician" (M.A. thesis, University of Arkansas, 1958), 25; Brough, "The Christian Advance in the University," *The New Ozark* (University of Arkansas, n.d., Brough Papers).

28. Crawford, "Charles Hillman Brough," 27.

29. Peggy Jacoway, *First Ladies of Arkansas* (Kingsport, Tenn.: Southern Publishers, Inc., 1941), 245–46; picture of home in BRS, Roll 1.

30. BRS, Roll 1; *Baptist Record,* 14 August 1884.

31. Brough to Anne Roark, 11 October 1907, 12 October 1907, 26 January 1908,

Brough Papers. Shortly before the wedding Anne received a letter from a friend who expressed amusement at the genteel professor's persistence in addressing his future bride as "Miss Anne." Years later, while on a speaking tour, Brough wrote her on the occasion of their fifteenth wedding anniversary, and called her "Miss Anne" in the closing paragraph. BRS, Roll 1; Brough to Anne Brough, Little Rock, 17 June 1923, Brough Papers.

32. Clippings from *Franklin* (Ky.) *Favorite,* n.d., and *Clinton Courier-Journal,* n.d., in BRS, Roll 1; Cora Brough to Anne Roark, 9 June 1908, and Charles Milton Brough (telegram) to Charles Hillman Brough, 17 June 1908, Brough Papers.

33. Anne Brough's handwritten account of wedding trip; Chautauqua program, Muskogee, Oklahoma (16–26 June 1908), BRS, Roll 1; Charles Milton Brough to Anne Brough, 14 August 1908, Brough Papers.

34. Charles Milton Brough to Hillman and Anne Brough, 17 November 1908; *Los Angeles Times,* 22 November 1910; telegram, Hillman Brough to Anne Brough, 18 November 1910; codicil to Charles Milton Brough's will, 1 December 1909, BRS, Roll 1.

35. University of Arkansas *Catalogue,* 1907–09, p. 9; Cook, "Charles Hillman Brough," 34; Widener, "The Political Campaign Speaking of Charles Hillman Brough in 1916 and 1932," 43.

36. Clipping from *Fayetteville Daily Democrat,* n.d., BRS, Roll 1.

Chapter 3

1. Arthur S. Link, "The Progressive Movement in the South, 1870–1914," *North Carolina Historical Review* 23 (January–October 1946): 172–95; Dewey W. Grantham, *Southern Progressivism: The Reconciliation of Progress and Tradition* (Knoxville, 1983), chs. 5–9.

2. John Ray Skates, *Mississippi: A Bicentennial History* (New York, 1979), 129–30; Richard L. Niswonger, *Arkansas Democratic Politics, 1896–1920* (Fayetteville: University of Arkansas Press, 1990), 228; Richard L. Watson Jr., "From Populism through the New Deal: Southern Political History," in John B. Boles and Evelyn Thomas Nolen, eds., *Interpreting Southern History: Historiographical Essays in Honor of Sanford W. Higginbotham* (Baton Rouge, 1987), 336; Jack Temple Kirby, "Westmoreland Davis: Progressive Insurgent," in Edward Younger, ed., *The Governors of Virginia, 1860–1978* (Charlottesville, Va., 1982), 215–17; Robert Sobel, ed., *Biographical Directory of the Governors of the United States, 1789–1978,* 4 vols., (Westport, Conn., 1978), III, 1152; ibid., IV, 1497.

3. Foy Lisenby, "Arkansas, 1900–1930," in *Historical Report of the Secretary of State of Arkansas,* ed. Winston Bryant (3 vols.; Little Rock, 1978), III, 141–42; Raymond Arsenault, *The Wild Ass of the Ozarks: Jeff Davis and the Social Bases of Southern Politics* (Knoxville: University of Tennessee Press, 1988), 3, 78–81.

4. Calvin R. Ledbetter Jr., *Carpenter from Conway: George Washington Donaghey as Governor of Arkansas, 1909–1913* (Fayetteville, Arkansas, 1993), ix; David Michael Moyers, "Arkansas Progressivism: The Legislative Record" (Ph.D. diss., University of Arkansas, 1986), 554, 557–58.

5. Ledbetter, *Carpenter from Conway*, 73–75; Lisenby, "Arkansas, 1900–1930," 143–44; Lisenby, "The First Meeting of the Arkansas Conference of Charities and Correction," *Arkansas Quarterly* 26 (Summer 1967): 154–61.

6. BRS, Roll 1; *Arkansas Gazette*, 3 May 1912; Grantham, *Southern Progressivism*, 374–75; *The Challenge of the Southern Sociological Congress* (Nashville, 1912); Brough, "The Work of the Commission of Southern Universities on the Race Question," *Annals of the Academy of Political and Social Science* 49 (September 1913), 47–57.

7. Leflar, *First One Hundred Years*, 80–81; Cook, "Arkansas's Charles Hillman Brough," 98.

8. Ibid.; Dewey W. Grantham, *The Life and Death of the Solid South: A Political History* (Lexington: University of Kentucky Press, 1988), 64; John B. Moore to Brough, 15 February 1913; Rev. Hay Watson Smith to Brough, 26 January 1913; Mims Williams to Brough, 10 January 1913, Brough Papers.

9. Brough, circular letter to "Dear Sir and Friend," 7 March 1913, Brough Papers; Cook, "Arkansas's Charles Hillman Brough," 94–95.

10. Brough, circular letter, 7 March 1913; Mims Williams to Brough, 10 January 1913; Judge J. S. Maples to Brough, 31 January 1913; T. T. Sheppard to Brough, 23 January 1913, Brough Papers.

11. *Arkansas Gazette*, 14 April 1913; George Brown Tindall, *The Emergence of the New South, 1913–1945* (Baton Rouge: Louisiana State University Press, 1967), 22; BRS, Roll 2; Cook, "Arkansas's Charles Hillman Brough," 102; Moyers, "Arkansas Progressivism," 554, 557–58.

12. Cook, "Arkansas's Charles Hillman Brough," 101; *Arkansas Gazette*, 6 June 1915; D. L. King to Brough, 23 November 1915; Albert Poff to Brough, 19 June 1915; Guy E. Williams to Brough, 7 June 1915; Booker Latimer to Brough, 30 May 1915; Benton County Teachers, copy of resolution, 3 June 1915, Brough Papers; BRS, Roll 2.

13. Charles W. Crawford, "From Classroom to State Capitol: Charles H. Brough and the Campaign of 1916," *Arkansas Historical Quarterly* 21 (Autumn 1962): 215; BRS, Roll 2; Richard L. Niswonger, *Arkansas Democratic Politics, 1896–1920* (Fayetteville: University of Arkansas Press, 1990), 337–39; Speech of Dr. C. H. Brough, Russellville, 29 November 1915, Brough Papers.

14. Niswonger, *Arkansas Democratic Politics*, 338–39; Joe T. Seagraves, "Arkansas Politics, 1874–1918" (Ph.D. diss., University of Kentucky, 1973), 371.

15. Cook, "Arkansas's Charles Hillman Brough," 109; Seagraves, "Arkansas Politics," 373; Brough, one-page reply to Earle W. Hodges, n.d., Brough Papers.

16. Williams to Brough, 7 February 1916; Venable to Brough, 8 February 1916; Womack, "Charles Hillman Brough," typewritten statement, 12 February 1916; W. T.

Lowrey, "To Whom It May Concern," typewritten statement, 15 February 1916, Brough Papers.

17. Brough, one-page reply to Hodges, n.d.; Brough, Speech, Russellville, 29 November 1915; "Reply of C. H. Brough to Earle W. Hodges," eleven-page statement, n.d., Brough Papers; Cook, "Arkansas's Charles Hillman Brough," 110; Extracts from C. H. Brough's Speeches in "His Candidacy for Governor: The Hays-Hodges Combine," sixteen-page pamphlet (Fort Smith, Ark., n.d.); The Brough Papers contain a one-page, untitled circular by "Smith and Brough supporters in East and South Arkansas," which indicates that Brough, or at least some of his supporters, also sought the votes of the "negrophobic" element. The circular, which also reflects anti-Catholic sentiments, included the charge that Hodges had Negroes managing his campaign in south and east Arkansas.

18. Affidavit of T. K. Falconer, 12 March 1916, Brough Papers; Cook, "Arkansas's Charles Hillman Brough," 111; D. L. King to J. W. House Jr., 23 November 1915, Brough Papers; Thomas W. Jackson, *On a Slow Train through Arkansaw*, ed. W. K. McNeil (Lexington: University of Kentucky Press, 1985). During his tenure as governor and beyond, Brough continued to defend Arkansas from Jackson and other detractors and to publicize and boost the state's resources and virtues. Chapter 6 deals more thoroughly with Brough's role in promoting a more positive image for Arkansas.

19. Brough, Speech, Russellville, 29 November 1915; G. T. Shrader to Brough, 28 March 1916, Brough Papers.

20. Niswonger, *Arkansas Democratic Politics*, 203–5.

21. Extracts from Speeches.

22. Niswonger, *Arkansas Democratic Politics*, 343; Crawford, "From Classroom to State Capitol," 225; State of Arkansas, *Journal of the House of Representatives, 1917*, p. 30.

Chapter 4

1. Ledbetter, *Carpenter from Conway*, 11.

2. *Arkansas Gazette*, 29 December 1916; *Fort Smith Times-Record*, 31 December 1916.

3. BRS, Roll 2.

4. Ibid.

5. For example, letters from Scipio Jones (14 November), A. Nelson (18 November), Samuel C. Mitchell (9 December), and J. R. Jewell (25 December), Brough Papers; BRS, Roll 2; *Arkansas Gazette*, 27 January 1917.

6. Fay Williams, *Arkansans of the Years*, 4 vols. (Little Rock: 1951–54), I, 62, 64.

7. *Arkansas Gazette*, 17 January 1917. The *Gazette* reported that the speech actually lasted two hours and ten minutes.

8. *House Journal, 1917,* pp. 27–67; BRS, Roll 2; *Arkansas Gazette,* 11 March 1917; *Arkansas Democrat,* 9 March 1917.

9. Granville Cubage to Brough, 17 November 1916; *House Journal, 1917,* p. 45; T. M. Stinnett and Clara B. Kennan, *All This and Tomorrow Too* (Little Rock, 1969), 126.

10. *House Journal, 1917,* p. 43; *Arkansas Democrat,* 2 January 1917; Moyers, "Arkansas Progressivism," 105–8; *Arkansas Gazette,* 18 February 1917; *Proceedings of the Arkansas Teachers Association* (Little Rock, 1917), 105.

11. Harry Lee Williams, *Behind the Scenes in Arkansas Politics* (Jonesboro, Ark., 1931), 143; *Arkansas Democrat Centennial Edition,* 1936, p. 35; BRS, Roll 2.

12. Foy Lisenby, "The Arkansas Conference on Charities and Correction, 1912–1937," *Arkansas Historical Quarterly* 29 (Spring 1970): 41–2; Lisenby, "Arkansas, 1900–1930," 146.

13. Erle Chambers, "Correctional Institutions," in David Y. Thomas, ed., *Arkansas and Its People: A History, 1541–1930* (4 vols.; New York, 1930), II, 499–500; *Arkansas Gazette,* 18 February 1917.

14. Niswonger, *Arkansas Democratic Politics,* 243, 246.

15. During the 1916 primary election Brough said he would not oppose woman suffrage if it was approved by the legislature. Crawford, "From Classroom to State Capitol," 219–20; *Arkansas Gazette,* 11 January 1917; A. Elizabeth Taylor, "The Woman Suffrage Movement in Arkansas," *Arkansas Historical Quarterly* 15 (Spring 1956): 29–30, 42, 46, 49.

16. *Arkansas Gazette,* 5 March 1917.

17. *Arkansas Gazette,* 7 March 1917; Lisenby, "Arkansas, 1900–1930," 147; Brough, "Address before the Biennial Meeting of the Federation of Women's Clubs, Hot Springs, Arkansas, 18 April 1918," Brough Papers.

18. *Arkansas Gazette,* 7 March 1917; Calvin R. Ledbetter Jr., "The Constitutional Convention of 1917–1918," *Arkansas Historical Quarterly* 34 (Spring 1975): 5–6, 8.

19. Larry Cook, "Charles Hillman Brough and the Good Roads Movement in Arkansas," *Ozark Historical Review* 6 (Spring 1977): 26–28; *Arkansas Gazette,* 11 January 1917; BRS, Roll 2.

20. *Arkansas Gazette,* 11 January and 24 January 1917; Niswonger, *Arkansas Democratic Politics,* 244; Moyers, "Arkansas Progressivism," 272–73.

21. BRS, Roll 3; *House Journal, 1919,* p. 34; *Arkansas Gazette,* 28 May and 7 April 1918; Brough to Lee York, 16 May 1918, Brough Papers.

22. BRS, Roll 3.

23. Ibid.; Brough to Walter G. Bowden, 26 July 1918; to Harry L. Ponder, 27 July 1918; to Charles Milton Brough III, 29 August 1918, Brough Papers.

24. *Report of the Arkansas State Council of Defense,* 22 May 1917 to 1 July 1919, pp. 5–8, 22–24; Gerald Senn, "Molders of Thought, Directors of Action: The Arkansas Council of Defense, 1917–1918," *Arkansas Historical Quarterly* 36 (Autumn 1977): 289–90; BRS, Roll 3.

25. Ledbetter, "Constitutional Convention," 5, 78; Moyers, "Arkansas Progressivism," 406–7.

26. Ledbetter, "Constitutional Convention," 14, 30, 33–34; BRS, Roll 3; Abe Collins, "Reminiscences of the Constitutional Convention of 1917–18," *Arkansas Historical Quarterly* 1 (1942): 117–21; *Arkansas Gazette,* 5 March 1919; *House Journal, 1921,* p. 81.

27. John R. Fordyce, "Notes on Routes and Ways of Travel in Arkansas," in *Arkansas Gazette Centennial Supplement, 1919,* pp. 47–49; *House Journal, 1919,* pp. 67–68, 85–86; Taylor, "Woman Suffrage Movement," 48–51; *Arkansas Gazette,* 3 August 1919.

28. *House Journal, 1919,* p. 88.

29. Ibid., 73; BRS, Roll 3; Chambers, "Correctional Institutions," 505.

30. J. L. Bond, "Public School Education in Arkansas," in *Arkansas Gazette Centennial Supplement, 1919,* p. 82.

31. To Cora Brough, 2 January 1919; to Mr. and Mrs. Wade Roark, 16 January 1919; to Knight Brough, 22 January 1919; to Mrs. Alice L. Brough, 30 July 1919; to Governor Simon Bamberger (Utah), 16 July 1919, Brough Papers. Actually Brough, beginning to feel better, postponed the hernia operation.

32. Brough to William C. Sproul (Penn.), 19 November 1919; to Carl E. Milleken (Maine), 19 November 1919; to Cora Brough, 17 November 1919, Brough Papers; copy of "Memorandum of Agreement," a contract dated September 1919, in possession of Price Roark of Little Rock; *Cabot Guard,* 19 September 1919.

33. Dr. C. C. Kirk to Brough, 16 March 1919; Brough to Dr. Shelby Greene, 2 July 1919; to Mr. and Mrs. Harry Anderson, 29 September 1919, Brough Papers; Crawford, "Charles Hillman Brough," 104.

34. *Journal of the Senate of Arkansas, 1919,* p. 68; Larry Cook, "Brough and the Good Roads Movement," 26; *Arkansas Gazette,* 2 October 1919 and 27 September 1919.

35. *Arkansas Gazette,* 2 October 1919; Arthur I. Waskow, *From Race Riot to Sit-In: 1919 and the 1960's* (Garden City, N.Y.: Doubleday & Co., 1967), 128; *Arkansas Democrat,* 2 October 1919; Harry Anderson to Brough, 7 October 1919, Brough Papers; *Arkansas Democrat,* 3 October 1919; BRS, Roll 3; Brough's secretary to W. A. McElroy, 7 October 1919, Brough Papers; George Brown Tindall, *The Emergence of the New South, 1913–1945* (Baton Rouge: Louisiana University Press, 1967), 153.

36. Walter White, *A Man Called White: The Autobiography of Walter White* (New York, 1948), 47–48; Richard C. Cortner, *A Mob Intent on Death: The naacp and the Arkansas Riot Cases* (Middleton, Conn., 1988), 36–37.

37. Brough, "Work of the Commission of Southern Universities on the Race Question"; Jones to Brough, 14 November 1916.

38. Brough, "Work of the Commission of Southern Universities on the Race Question," 154; Lisenby, "Arkansas, 1900–1930," 149.

39. *Arkansas Gazette,* 26 November 1919; Arkansas Advancement Association,

Are You Interested in Arkansas? (Little Rock, 1921; a pamphlet in possession of Price Roark of Little Rock).

40. BRS, Roll 3.

41. Ibid.

42. Ibid.; W. David Baird, "Thomas Chipman McRae," in Donovan and Gatewood, eds., *Governors of Arkansas: Essays in Political Biography* (Fayetteville: University of Arkansas Press, 1981), 155. Chapter 6 contains further discussion of the *New York Times* coverage of problems associated with the road improvement districts in Arkansas.

43. Widener, "The Political Campaign Speaking of Charles Hillman Brough," 54; BRS, Roll 3; Widener, "Charles Hillman Brough," *Arkansas Historical Quarterly* 34 (Summer 1975): 115.

44. Cook, "Arkansas's Charles Hillman Brough," 126–7; Brough to P. C. Allan, 23 September 1919; to Mr. and Mrs. Harry Anderson, 29 September 1919, Brough Papers.

45. BRS, Roll 3.

Chapter 5

1. BRS, Roll 1.

2. Ibid.; *Arkansas Gazette,* 22 March 1921.

3. BRS, Roll 3; *Arkansas Gazette,* 30 March 1921 and 1 April 1921.

4. *Arkansas Gazette,* 13 May 1921; BRS, Roll 4.

5. Brough to Pettie, 15 July 1921; Pettie to Brough, 19 July 1921, Brough Papers.

6. Cook, *Arkansas's Charles Hillman Brough,* 153; BRS, Roll 1; Widener, "The Political Campaign Speaking of Charles Hillman Brough," 57.

7. Brough to Pettie, 15 July 1921, Brough Papers.

8. The work of the association will be treated more fully in the next chapter.

9. BRS, Roll 4.

10. Ibid.

11. BRS, Rolls 1 and 4.

12. Theodore Morrison, *Chautauqua: A Center for Education, Religion, and the Arts in America* (New York, 1974), 161, 176–78; John S. Noffsinger, *Correspondence Schools, Lyceums, Chautauquas* (New York, 1926), 126–27.

13. Victoria Case and Robert Ormond Case, *We Called It Culture: The Story of Chautauqua* (Garden City, N.Y., 1948), 71; Morrison, *Chautauqua,* 181; Bruce Bliven, "Nearest the Hearts of Ten Million," *Collier's* (8 September 1923), 6–7; Alma and Paul Ellerbe, *The Most American Thing in America* (World's Work, vol. 48, August 1924), 441; Bliven, "Mother, Home, and Heaven," *New Republic* (9 January 1924), 173–75.

14. Case and Case, *We Called It Culture,* 72, 75; Harry P. Harrison and Karl

William Detzer, *Culture under Canvas: The Story of Tent Chautauqua* (New York, 1958), 144.

15. Crawford, "Charles Hillman Brough," 110; BRS, Roll 1; Elizabeth Bentley Bierwirth, "A Rhetorical and Semantic Study of Charles Hillman Brough's Major Chautauqua Address" (M.A. thesis, University of Arkansas, 1959), 4; Widener, "The Political Campaign Speaking of Charles Hillman Brough," 59.

16. *Arkansas Gazette,* 30 September 1923; Bierwirth, "Rhetorical and Semantic Study," 42, 45.

17. Bierwirth, "Rhetorical and Semantic Study," 42; BRS, Roll 1; S. C. Parish to Brough, 1 August 1925, Brough Papers.

18. Brough to S. C. Sorensen, 29 December 1923, Brough Papers; to W. I. Atkinson, 29 November 1924, Brough Papers.

19. BRS, Roll 5; *Arkansas Democrat,* 25 June 1924.

20. BRS, Roll 5.

21. A. M. Weiskoff to Brough, 30 July 1924, Brough Papers; Brough to Carl Backman, 30 November 1923, Brough Papers.

22. Robert F. Ferrante to Brough, 21 February 1924, and 11 March 1924, Brough Papers.

23. BRS, Roll 5; Brough to W. I. Atkinson, 29 January 1925, Brough Papers; Charles E. Dicken to Brough, 19 February 1925; Alma Futrell to Brough, 14 March 1925, Brough Papers.

24. Brough to Mrs. E. H. Abbington, 19 March 1925; Brough to O. E. Holmes, 2 April 1925; Brough to Mr. and Mrs. A. M. Lund, 13 May 1925; Doak S. Campbell to Brough, 24 March 1925; Charles Dicken to Brough, 24 April 1925, Brough Papers.

25. Brough to A. J. Reap, 7 April 1925; Brough to Dr. R. T. Cook, 16 May 1925; Brough to W. V. Harrison, 16 May 1925; George C. Whitehead to Mrs. Brough, 23 May 1925, Brough Papers.

26. Brough to George C. Whitehead, 15 July 1925; Redpath Chautauqua to Employers' Indemnity Company, Kansas City, Missouri, 24 July 1925; Brough to M. L. Martin, 24 July 1925; S. A. Lane to Brough, 24 May 1926; Brough to E. J. White, 9 December 1926; R. I. Brown to Owen D. Young, 1 February 1926, Brough Papers.

Chapter 6

1. Copy of contract, dated 1919, in possession of Price Roark of Little Rock; *Cabot Guard,* 19 September 1919.

2. BRS, Roll 1.

3. *Mississippi College Magazine* 6 (March 1900): 13; vol. 7 (January 1901): 6, 10.

4. BRS, Roll 1; address to Arkansas Teachers' Association, Little Rock, 1917, Brough Papers.

5. Jackson, *On a Slow Train through Arkansaw;* Mary Fortner, "Opie Read—

Arkansas' 'Mark Twain' of the Ozarks," *Arkansas Democrat Sunday Magazine,* 28 May 1944.

6. BRS, Roll 1.

7. Address to Missouri Bar Association, 20 September 1918, Brough Papers.

8. In his inaugural addresses, as well as in other messages to the legislature, Brough frequently noted that "all but [six states, seven states, etc.]" have instituted a particular reform, or established a certain agency.

9. *Arkansas Gazette Centennial Supplement,* 20 November 1919.

10. Edgar Kemler, *The Irreverent Mr. Mencken* (Boston, 1950), 176; William Manchester, *H. L. Mencken: Disturber of the Peace* (New York, 1950), 123; Carl R. Dolmetisch, *The Smart Set: A History and Anthology* (New York, 1966), 245.

11. *New York Times,* 26 and 27 March 1921.

12. Ibid., 26 March 1921; *Arkansas Gazette,* 30 March 1921.

13. Brough to Pettie, 15 July 1921, Brough Papers.

14. Alexis Wade Schwitalia, *Who's Who in Little Rock, 1921* (Little Rock: Who's Who Publishers, 1921), 107; copy of petition for incorporation of Arkansas Advancement Association, with By-laws of the Association, 1921, in possession of Price Roark of Little Rock; *Arkansas Gazette,* 18 July 1921; Pettie to Brough, 19 July 1921.

15. Arkansas Advancement Association, *Are You Interested in Arkansas?*

16. Ibid.

17. Brough, "The New Arkansas," *Candid Opinion* (January 1922), 169–70.

18. Ibid., 170.

19. Ibid., 171.

20. Ibid.

21. *Congressional Record* (House of Representatives), 13 May 1922, 6895.

22. Ibid., 6895–99.

23. Brough to Burton D. Hurd, 16 November 1923, Brough Papers; *Arkansas Gazette,* 17 November 1923 and 30 November 1923; BRS, Roll 5.

24. *Journal of the Senate of Arkansas,* 44th General Assembly, 1923, 15–16.

25. *The Nation* 116 (May 1923): 515–17.

26. Address to visiting Kansas City delegation and the Little Rock Board of Commerce, 16 April 1924; *Arkansas Utility News,* 26 January 1926; Hodges to Brough, 26 February 1925, Brough Papers; BRS, Roll 5; *Arkansas Democrat,* 16 June 1929; *Arkansas: The Commonwealth of Opportunity and Achievement,* published text of Brough's radio address over KMOX, St. Louis, July 1929, Brough Papers.

27. BRS, Roll 6; *Collier's,* 29 March 1930, 4.

28. Donald Holley, "Arkansas in the Great Depression," in *Historical Report of the Secretary of State, Arkansas* (Little Rock, 1978) III, 159; *Literary Digest* (28 February 1931), 5.

29. *Literary Digest* (28 February 1931), 6; *Baltimore Evening Sun,* 19 January, 16 February, 10 February 1931; *Journal of the House of Representatives of Arkansas, 1931,* 990–993.

30. *Journal of the House of Representatives of Arkansas, 1931*, 991.

31. Ibid., 993.

32. "The Case for Arkansas," *Baltimore Evening Sun*, 16 February 1931; Brough to Mencken, 24 February 1931, Brough Papers.

33. Mencken to Brough, 31 March and 7 April 1931, Brough Papers.

34. *Vanity Fair* (September 1933), 14, 57.

35. Brough to Brokaw, 29 August, 8 September, and 9 September 1933, Brough Papers; personal interview with Richard C. Butler, Little Rock, 30 April 1990.

Chapter 7

1. John W. Moncrief to Brough, 13 August 1927.

2. *Polk's Little Rock City Directory,* 1926, p. 121, and 1928, p. 112; R. I. Brown to Brough, 12 May 1926, Brough Papers; Brough, "The Business Outlook for Arkansas in 1926," *Arkansas Utility News,* 1; "Synopsis of Address by Dr. Charles Hillman Brough before Biennial Conference of Boy Scout Executives of Boy Scouts of America," 26 September 1926, Brough Papers; Brough to Dr. J. W. Provine, 2 November 1926, Brough Papers; Brough to Jo Frauenthal, 6 December 1926, Brough Papers.

3. Brough to J. C. Futrall, 13 September 1926; to Minnie U. Rutherford-Fuller, 30 September 1926, Brough Papers.

4. BRS, Roll 5; Brough to Cora Brough, 17 September 1927; to John C. Futrall, 6 June 1927; to Joe T. Robinson, 8 June 1927, Brough Papers.

5. Brough to Charles Brough, 6 June 1927; to Knight Brough, 16 June and 17 September 1927; to Charles Brough, 16 November; to Cora Brough, 17 September 1927, Brough Papers; BRS, Roll 5; Hodges to Brough, 28 September 1927, Brough Papers.

6. (Conway) *Log Cabin Democrat,* 18 April 1928; *Central Baptist College Quarterly Bulletin* 14 (29 May 1928): 10; *Log Cabin Democrat,* 30 May and 11 July 1928; Brough to Lyford Harper, 14 July 1928, Brough Papers; interview with Daisy Bruce, Fayetteville, Arkansas, 2 December 1971; *Log Cabin Democrat,* 17 July 1928.

7. E. L. Haney to Brough, 20 July 1928; J. W. Ramsey to Brough, 18 July 1928; Brough to Rev. Ben Cox, 20 July 1928; to Herbert D. Russell, 20 July 1928; H. L. Turner to Brough, 14 July 1928, Brough Papers.

8. *Arkansas Democrat,* 13 September 1928; *Log Cabin Democrat,* 18 September 1928.

9. *Log Cabin Democrat,* 18 September 1928.

10. Brough had served as a Baptist deacon at both Fayetteville and Little Rock, and as a vice-president of the Southern Baptist Convention. In addition he had "filled pulpits" from time to time, and had given speeches and written articles supportive of Christian ideals.

11. Brough to Bishop Winchester, 20 July 1928, Brough Papers; Nevin Emil Neal, "A Biography of Joseph T. Robinson" (Ph.D. diss. University of Oklahoma, 1958), 289.

12. Brough to Millard E. Tydings, 28 September 1928, Brough Papers; *Centralian,* 21 September 1928.

13. *Baptist Advance* 27 (4 October 1928): 1; R. H. Dudley to Brough, 27 September 1928, Brough Papers.

14. *Baptist Advance* 27 (4 October 1928): 1.

15. Ibid.; *Baptist Advance* 27 (11 October 1928): 3.

16. Ruth Tucker to Brough, 8 October 1928; Brough to Tucker, 10 October and 22 October 1928, Brough Papers.

17. BRS, Roll 5.

18. Ibid.; *Log Cabin Democrat,* 29 October 1928.

19. BRS, Roll 6; Brough to R. T. Cook Jr., 31 October 1928, Brough Papers.

20. BRS, Roll 6; *Log Cabin Democrat,* 1 November 1928; *Arkansas Gazette,* 2 November 1928; letters of appreciation from Brough (October 30 and 31) to the following: Charles D. Frierson, J. D. Thweatt, I. E. Moore, John and Dougald McMillen, and Griffin Smith. Brough Papers.

21. Brough to Jason L. Light, 16 July 1928, Brough Papers; BRS, Roll 6; Brough to Thaddeus Caraway, 14 June 1929, Brough Papers.

22. *Acts of Arkansas, 1929,* 1518–19; Rev. Hay Watson Smith to Brough, 11 May 1928; Brough to Reverend Smith, 30 April 1928; Futrall to Brough, 24 January 1928, Brough Papers.

23. *Arkansas Baptist Annual,* 1924, pp. 66–67; *Baptist Advance* (25 October 1928): 2; *Baptist Advance* (1 November 1928): 1, 4.

24. Acts of Arkansas, 1929, 1519; Brough to Homer L. Pearson, 9 November 1928, Brough Papers.

25. Between October 31 and November 13 he wrote to potential supporters in Berryville, Stuttgart, El Dorado, Little Rock, Paragould, Texarkana, Pine Bluff, Warren, and Lonoke. The quotation is from a letter to Rev. W. H. Gregory at Lonoke, 5 November 1928, Brough Papers.

26. *Arkansas Gazette,* 17 November and 23 November 1928; clipping from *Texarkana Evening News,* 22 November 1928, in BRS, Roll 6; *Arkansas Baptist Annual,* 1928, p. 79.

27. BRS, Roll 6; *Baptist Advance* 27 (13 December 1928): 1, and vol. 28 (17 January 1929): 4; *Arkansas Gazette,* 17 March 1929; *Centralian,* 16 March 1929, 1; *Arkansas Gazette,* 3 May and 16 March 1929.

28. *Centralian,* 16 March 1929, 1.

29. Ibid.; Robinson to Brough, 15 February 1929, Brough Papers.

30. *Arkansas Democrat,* 23 June 1929; Brough to Alex Washburn, 25 June 1929, Brough Papers.

31. Brough to Futrall, 19 June 1929; Robert Morton Angus to Brough, 17 June 1929, Brough Papers; "Arkansas: The Commonwealth of Opportunity and

Achievement," mimeographed copy of address delivered by Brough on 27 June 1929, Brough Papers. A printed copy of this speech, dated 1931, is also in the Brough collection; BRS, Rolls 6 and 7.

32. BRS, Roll 6; Brough to J. C. Futrall, 19 June 1929; to Granville Roark, 25 June 1929, Brough Papers.

33. BRS, Roll 6.

34. *Arkansas Democrat,* 23 June 1929; BRS, Roll 6; Brough to Alex Washburn, 25 June 1929, Brough Papers.

35. BRS, Roll 7; to W. E. Mullins, 26 March 1929, Brough Papers; BRS, Roll 6; Brough to Futrall, 19 June 1929, Brough Papers.

36. BRS, Roll 7.

37. BRS, Roll 6.

38. Ibid.

Chapter 8

1. David Malone, *Hattie and Huey: An Arkansas Tour* (Fayetteville: University of Arkansas Press, 1989), 2.

2. McClellan to Brough, 7 November 1931, Brough Papers; Diane D. Kincaid, *Silent Hattie Speaks: The Personal Journal of Senator Hattie Caraway* (Westport, Conn.: Greenwood Press, 1979), 6–7.

3. Kincaid, *Silent Hattie Speaks,* 6; T. Harry Williams, *Huey Long: A Biography* (New York: Alfred A. Knopf, 1969), 584.

4. Kincaid, *Silent Hattie Speaks,* 7–8.

5. Ibid., 75–76.

6. P. P. Boggan to Brough, 25 February 1932 (copy of letter in possession of Price Roark of Little Rock, nephew of Anne Brough); F. D. Allen to Brough, 2 March 1932, Brough Papers; BRS, Roll 7.

7. Newspaper clipping, n.d., BRS, Roll 7.

8. Ibid.

9. Clipping from *Warren* (Ark.) *Eagle-Democrat,* 13 February 1930, BRS, Roll 7.

10. *Arkansas Democrat,* 10 March 1932.

11. Supporters who wrote Brough in March 1932 included W. W. Campbell, a Forrest City banker; Lucien Coleman, a Lepanto lawyer; W. A. McKeowen, a Glenwood businessman; and W. B. Snipes, an Aubrey doctor. The first three are in the Brough Papers, the last two are in possession of Price Roark. Other Arkansans who wrote letters of support and appreciation in the ensuing weeks included Robert Joseph Brown of Little Rock (to Mrs. Brough), Mrs. J. D. Head of Texarkana, Dr. E. B. Milburn of Calico Rock, and Frank A. Lee of Vanderwoort. Brough Papers. Out-of-state support was expressed by V. L. Webb of Texarkana, Texas, and Riley C. Armstrong of Houston, Texas. Courtesy of Price Roark.

12. Brough to Judge and Mrs. J. S. Lake, 4 April 1932, courtesy of Price Roark; Brough to D. H. Hastings, 18 April 1932, Brough Papers; Dr. Edward C. McDaniel to Brough, 18 June 1932, courtesy of Price Roark.

13. Dr. Robert B. Corney to Brough, 22 April 1932; W. O. Jacobs to Brough, 25 May 1932; W. K. Oldham to Brough, 6 June 1932; Ben K. Wheeler to Brough, 12 July 1932, Brough Papers.

14. Ella E. Rockwell to Brough, 12 July 1932; Mrs. J. D. Head to Brough, 8 May 1932; Frank A. Lee to Brough, 11 May 1932; Dr. E. B. Milburn to Brough, 28 April 1932, Brough Papers; clipping from *Memphis Commercial Appeal*, 2 July 1932, in BRS, Roll 7.

15. Brough to W. W. Campbell, 31 March 1932, courtesy of Price Roark; Brough to Dr. G. W. Puryear, 30 May 1932, Brough Papers.

16. A. J. Jeffries to Brough, 9 July 1932, Brough Papers; Malone, *Hattie and Huey,* 11–12; *Harrison* (Ark.) *Daily Times,* 3 June 1932; Dr. F. E. Baker to Brough, 29 June 1932; Tom McGill to Brough, 29 June 1932; Steele Kennedy to Brough, 13 July 1932, Brough Papers; *Harrison Daily Times,* 10 May 1932; Brough to Judge A. L. Hutchins, 11 May 1932, courtesy of Price Roark; Gustave Jones to Benton Kitchens (Brough's campaign director), 30 July 1932, Brough Papers.

17. Newspaper clipping on Brough's speech at Magnolia, 7 July 1932; newspaper account of J. S. Utley's introduction of Brough at Little Rock, n.d., BRS, Roll 7; Abe and Ollie Collins to Anne Brough, n.d., Brough Papers; "Lyford" to Dr. and Mrs. Brough, 25 May 1932, courtesy of Price Roark.

18. Clippings from Piggott and Paragould newspapers, 4 and 5 July, respectively, and from Fayetteville Daily Democrat, n.d., in BRS, Roll 7; Arkansas Gazette, 6 July 1932.

19. Clipping from unidentified newspaper; clipping from *Fayetteville Daily Democrat,* n.d.; clipping from *Magnolia Banner-News,* 7 July 1932; BRS, Roll 7.

20. Newspaper account of J. S. Utley's introduction of Brough at Little Rock, 28 July 1932; newspaper account of Brough's speech at Magnolia, 7 July 1932, in BRS, Roll 7; F. A. Humphreys to Brough, 1 April 1932; Abe and Ollie Collins to Mrs. Brough, n.d., Brough Papers.

21. J. S. Utley's introduction of Brough at Little Rock, 28 July 1932; unidentified newspaper clipping; clipping from (Pine Bluff) *Jefferson County Progress,* 15 July 1932 (reprinted from *De Queen Bee,* 1 July 1932), BRS, Roll 7.

22. J. S. Utley's introduction of Brough at Little Rock, 28 July 1932; unidentified clipping; newspaper account of Brough's speech at Magnolia, 7 July 1932, BRS, Roll 7; *Arkansas Gazette,* 31 July 1932.

23. Brough, in a letter to Judge A. L. Hutchins of Forrest City, noted that Mrs. Caraway's personal friends were surprised at her entrance into the race and that the great majority of her friends and those of her late husband advised her against it. Griffin Smith of Mariana, writing to Mrs. Caraway (1 June 1932), painted a discouraging picture of her prospects of winning. Griffin Smith Papers, History Commission, Little Rock.

24. *Arkansas Gazette,* 20 July 1932; *Harrison Daily Times,* 20 July 1932.

25. Stuart Towns, "A Louisiana Medicine Show: The Kingfish Elects an Arkansas Senator," *Arkansas Historical Quarterly* 25 (Summer 1966): 121–22; *Harrison Daily Times,* 12 May 1932.

26. *Arkansas Gazette,* 2 August 1932; Gustave Jones to Kitchens, 30 July 1932, Brough Papers.

27. Williams, *Huey Long,* 583–93, 591.

28. *Arkansas Gazette,* 4 August 1932; Malone, *Hattie and Huey,* 94; *Log Cabin Democrat,* 3 August 1932; *Arkansas Gazette,* 8 August 1932 (political advertisement); *Arkansas Gazette,* 9 August 1932 (political advertisement); L. J. Bryson to Brough, 8 August 1932, courtesy of Price Roark.

29. Towns, "Louisiana Medicine Show," 126; *Arkansas Gazette,* 11 August 1932; *Harrison Daily Times,* 10 August 1932.

30. "Ray" (a Fort Smith businessman) to Brough, 12 August 1932, courtesy of Price Roark; Karr S. Shannon, "Brough Was a Mental Giant," *Arkansas Democrat Magazine,* 11 December 1960; letters to Brough through 13 August by the following: E. F. Edwards, Wiley Lin Hurie, E. M. Ratliff, J. W. Moore, Gertrude MacChesney, Charles D. Johnson, all of these letters in possession of Price Roark.

31. E. F. Edwards to Brough, 12 August 1932, courtesy of Price Roark.

32. Brough to Roosevelt, 9 December 1932, Brough Papers. Cook, "Arkansas's Charles Hillman Brough," 174–75; Cook cites Ralph Widener's article, "The Political Campaign Speaking of Charles Hillman Brough in 1916 and 1932," and an "anonymous Brough contemporary."

33. Brough to Mrs. Caraway, 9 November 1932, courtesy of Price Roark.

Chapter 9

1. Brough to O. E. Rayburn, 5 October 1932; to Dr. Felix Gaudin, 1 February 1934; to William D. Gray, 25 September 1935, Brough Papers.

2. Brough to Stella S. Center, 11 August 1932; Sol Bloom to Brough, 31 May 1934; Brough to Rev. Arthur A. Dulaney, 14 March 1934; to C. A. Cunningham, 27 March 1935; to Roger William Straus, 21 October 1935; to George Fort Milton, 20 June 1935; to Dr. [Douglas] Southall Freeman, 22 October 1935; to Miss Fenton Utley, 16 October 1935; David F. Houston to Brough, 7 October 1932; Brough to Mrs. Minnie U. Fuller, 22 September 1932, Brough Papers.

3. *Arkansas Gazette,* 18 September 1932; interview with Dr. George Thompson, Conway, Arkansas, 25 April 1993; Cook, "Arkansas's Charles Hillman Brough," 175.

4. Brough to John N. Garner, 9 November 1932; Franklin D. Roosevelt to Brough, 9 December 1932; Brough, "Address . . . at Kansas City and Other Missouri and Kansas Points, October 15th to 22nd, Inclusive," copy of typescript speech, Brough Papers.

5. Guy T. Helvering to Brough, 11 November 1932, Brough Papers.

6. Brough to Garner, 9 November 1932; to Roosevelt, 9 December 1932, Brough Papers.

7. As noted in the previous chapter, Brough had been obliged to run his senatorial campaign "on a shoestring." This was partly the result of the high cost of his illnesses in the 1920s, and partly because Brough, despite his expertise in economics, had not been particularly prudent with his money. Interview with Price Roark (Anne Brough's nephew), Little Rock, 14 August 1987.

8. C. M. Hirst to Robinson, 23 February 1933; J. W. Burnett to Brough, 25 March 1933; Robinson to Marion Wesson, 10 April 1933, Brough Papers.

9. Brough to Morris Minor, 7 August 1933; to J. B. Johns, 31 January 1934; Utley to President Roosevelt, 10 February 1934, Brough Papers.

10. Brough to George Fort Milton, 20 June 1935, Brough Papers; BRS, Roll 7; H.R. 6228, 73d Congress, 2d sess., 1934, in Brough Papers.

11. Brough, telegram to Anne Brough, 27 March 1934, Brough Papers.

12. Brough to Tom B. Meglemry, 21 September 1934; to R. B. Smith, 13 July 1934; to George Fort Milton, 20 June 1935, Brough Papers. In other correspondence Brough gives different estimates of the value of the property in dispute. Brough to Mr. and Mrs. J. R. Wilson, 8 April 1935, and to Mr. and Mrs. John L. Carter, 19 September 1935, Brough Papers.

13. Brough to Dr. and Mrs. John W. Inzer, 11 March 1935; Boundary Commission, *District of Columbia and Virginia Boundary Line* (Washington: Government Printing Office, 1936), Brough Papers; BRS, Roll 7; *Congressional Record,* 74th Congress, 2d sess., vol. 8, Part I, 1936, passim.

14. Brough to A. W. Parke, 16 June 1934; to Mrs. Lessie Stringfellow Read, 22 September 1934; to Dr. Jacob Hollander, 27 June 1934; to Edward L. Alexander, 11 October 1934; Conway Hail to Dr. and Mrs. Brough, 5 August 1935; Allsopp to Brough, 29 May 1935, Brough Papers.

15. Brooks Hays to Brough, 20 June 1934; William L. Humphries to Brough, 22 November 1934; Brough to Fred T. Wilson, 9 November 1934, Brough Papers; interview with Richard C. Butler, Little Rock, Arkansas, 30 April 1990; Brough to J. Merrick Moore, 19 November 1934, Brough Papers.

16. Brough to George W. Donaghey, 28 January 1935; to W. M. Greeson, 18 June 1935; to Mrs. Lessie Stringfellow Read, 26 July 1935; clipping of letter from Brough to the "People's Column" of the *Arkansas Gazette,* 2 November 1935, Brough Papers.

17. Brough to L. S. Dunaway, 15 September 1934; to R. B. Smith, 13 July 1934; to Fred T. Wilson, 9 November 1934; to A. W. Parke, 16 June 1934; to Dr. and Mrs. John W. Inzer, 11 March 1935; to Mr. and Mrs. Robert Hutchinson, 5 June 1935; to Charles H. Ray, 12 August 1935; to Dr. S. P. McConnell, 4 October 1935; to Miss Fenton Utley, 16 October 1935; to Mr. and Mrs. J. R. Wilson, 8 April 1935, Brough Papers.

18. Brough to L. S. Dunaway, 15 September 1934; to Dr. S. P. McConnell, 4 October 1935; "Synopsis of Address . . . Before the Architects Club," 1 January 1935, Brough Papers; BRS, Roll 7; Brough to John Rust, 20 September 1935, Brough Papers;

Arkansas Gazette, 5 July 1934; Brough to Dr. Edward L. Alexander, 19 October 1934; Grover C. Jones, telegram to Brough, 31 October 1934; Brough to Dan W. Weggland, 7 November 1934; to Joseph J. McMunn, 10 January 1935; to Mr. and Mrs. J. R. Wilson, 8 April 1935, Brough Papers; *Arkansas Gazette,* 9 September 1935; Brough to W. M. Greeson, 18 June 1935, Brough Papers.

19. *Arkansas Gazette,* 5 July 1934; Utley to Dr. and Mrs. Brough, 29 June 1934, Brough Papers.

20. E. K. Ruple to Brough, 27 June 1934, Brough Papers; *Arkansas Gazette,* 7 July 1934.

21. BRS, Roll 7.

22. *Arkansas Gazette,* 27 December 1935; BRS, Roll 7; Harding to Anne Brough, 27 December 1935; V. C. Kays, telegram to Anne Brough, 26 December 1935, Brough Papers.

23. *Arkansas Gazette,* 27, 29, and 30 December 1935.

Epilogue

1. BRS, Roll 1; Williams, *Arkansans of the Years,* I, 62.

2. Cook, "Arkansas's Charles Hillman Brough," 24; Dr. S. Otho Hesterly to author, 31 January 1994.

3. M. P. Hunt, *The Story of My Life* (Louisville, Ky., 1941), 101.

4. *Arkansas Democrat,* 11 December 1960.

5. Williams, *Arkansans of the Years,* I, 64.

6. Telephone conversation between the author and Harry L. Ponder, 27 November 1993; Brough to Mrs. Brough, 17 June 1923.

7. Bierwirth, "Rhetorical and Semantic Study," 88.

Appendix

1. Brough Papers.

2. Ibid.

3. Ibid.

4. Ibid.

5. As quoted in Bierwith, "A Rhetorical and Semantic Study," 51–52.

Bibliography

Primary Sources

Manuscript Collections

Charles Hillman Brough Papers, University of Arkansas, Mullins Library, Special Collections, Fayetteville, Ark.

John C. Futrall Papers, University of Arkansas, Mullins Library, Special Collections, Fayetteville, Ark.

Joseph T. Robinson Papers, University of Arkansas, Mullins Library, Special Collections, Fayetteville, Ark.

Griffin Smith Papers, Arkansas History Commission, Little Rock, Ark.

Brough-Roark Scrapbooks, General Microfilm File, History Commission, Little Rock, Arkansas

Roll 1: 1876–1935.
Roll 2: 1913–1917.
Roll 3: 1918–1920.
Roll 4: 1921–1924.
Roll 5: 1924–1928.
Roll 6: 1928–1930.
Roll 7: 1929–1932.

Interviews

Daisy Bruce, Fayetteville, 2 December 1971.
Richard C. Butler, Little Rock, 30 April 1990.
Evadna Roark, Little Rock, 14 August 1987.
Price Roark, Little Rock, 14 August 1987.
George Thompson, Conway, 25 April 1993.
Mrs. George F. Trapp, North Little Rock, 17 August 1987.

Public Documents

Acts of Arkansas, 1917, 1919.
Arkansas, *Biennial Report, Secretary of State, 1921–1924.*
Arkansas, *Journal of the House of Representatives of Arkansas,* 1917, 1919, 1923, 1931.

Arkansas, *Journal of the Senate of Arkansas*, 1917, 1919.

Congressional Record, 1922 and 1936.

Report of the Arkansas State Council of Defense, May 22, 1917 to July 1, 1919.

United States Census, 1870, 1880, 1900.

Reports and Proceedings

Arkansas Baptist State Convention, *Proceedings*, 1924 and 1928.

Arkansas State Teachers' Association, *Forty-Fifth Annual Session*, Little Rock,
   December 1912.

Riley, Franklin S., ed. *Publications of the Mississippi Historical Society*, Oxford, Miss.,
   1899 and 1900.

Books, Pamphlets, and Articles

Arkansas Advancement Association. *Are You Interested in Arkansas?* Little Rock,
   1921.

The Arkansas Teacher, February 1914.

Baptist Advance, 4 October–28 November 1928.

Bond, J. L. "Public School Education in Arkansas." *Arkansas Gazette Centennial
   Edition*, 1919.

Brough, Charles Hillman. *Arkansas, The Commonwealth of Opportunity and
   Achievement*. Little Rock, Ark., 1931.

———. "The Clinton Riot." *Publications of the Mississippi Historical Society* 6
   (1902): 53–63.

———. *Extracts from Charles Hillman Brough's Speeches in His Candidacy for
   Governor of Arkansas: The Hays-Hodges Combine*. Fort Smith, Ark., n.d.

———. "Historic Homes of Arkansas." *Arkansas Historical Association, Publications*
   1 (1906): 286–99.

———. "History of Taxation in Mississippi." *Publications of the Mississippi
   Historical Society* 2 (1899): 113–24.

———. "The Ideal Student." *University of Mississippi Magazine* 25 (December
   1901): 5–9.

———. *Irrigation in Utah*. Baltimore: Johns Hopkins University Press, 1898.

———. "Loyalty to Mississippi." *Mississippi College Magazine* 6 (March 1900): 4–15.

———. "The New Arkansas." *Candid Opinion*, January 1922, 169–71.

———. "A Plea for the Extension of the Rural Free School Term." *Mississippi
   College Magazine* 9 (October 1902): 3–17.

———. "We Study But to Serve." *Mississippi College Magazine* 7 (January 1901):
   1–12.

———. "Work of the Commission of Southern Universities on the Race Question."
   Annals of the American Academy of Political and Social Science 49 (September
   1913): 47–57.

Donaghey, George Washington. *Autobiography.* Benton, Ark., 1939.
Hunt, M. P. *The Story of My Life.* Louisville, Ky., 1941.
Edson, C. L. "Arkansas: A Native Proletariat." *Nation,* 2 May 1923, 515–17.
Oliver, Travis Y. "Hell's Fire—Arkansas!" *Vanity Fair,* September 1933, 14 and 57.
Pettie, Virgil C. "The Arkansas Advancement Association: Its Object and Purpose."
    Candid Opinion, September 1921, 101–2.
Weathersby, H. M. "Alumni Department." *Mississippi College Magazine* 10 (February
    1904): 23–25.
White, Walter. *A Man Called White: The Autobiography of Walter White.* New York,
    1948.
Williams, Harry Lee. *Behind the Scenes in Arkansas Politics.* Jonesboro, Ark., 1931.

Miscellaneous Primary Sources

Central Baptist College. *Quarterly Bulletin, 1926–27.*
———. *Quarterly Bulletin, 1928–29.*
Haefeli, Lee, and Frank J. Cannon. *Directory of Ogden City and Weber County.*
    Ogden City, Utah: Ogden Herald Publishing Company, 1883.
Hobart, H. B. *Ogden City Directory for 1890.* Salt Lake City: Kelly & Company, 1890.
Little Rock City Directory, 1917–1935.
Mississippi College. *Annual Catalogue, 1898–1899.* Brandon, Miss.: E. B. Tabor, 1899.
Ogden City Directory for 1892–1893. Ogden, Utah: R. L. Polk & Company, 1892.
Ogden City Directory, 1895–96. R. L. Polk & Company, 1896.
Subject File, Mississippi Department of Archives and History, Jackson, Miss.
University of Arkansas. *The Cardinal,* vol. 6 (1904–05).
———. *Catalogue,* 1905–06.
———. *The Razorback,* 1916 and 1917.

Secondary Sources

Books and Articles

Arsenault, Raymond Ostby. *The Wild Ass of the Ozarks.* Philadelphia: Temple
    University Press, 1984.
Barnes, H. F. *Among Arkansas Leaders.* Little Rock, 1934.
Baxley, Thomas L. "Prison Reforms during the Donaghey Administration."
    Arkansas Historical Quarterly 22 (Spring 1963): 76–84.
Boles, John B., and Evelyn Thomas Nolen, eds. *Interpreting Southern History:
    Historiographical Essays in Honor of Sanford W. Higginbotham.* Baton Rouge,
    1987.
Braden, Waldo W. *The Oral Tradition in the South.* Baton Rouge: Louisiana State
    University Press, 1983.

Butts, J. W., and Dorothy James. "The Underlying Causes of the Elaine Riot of 1919." *Arkansas Historical Quarterly* 20 (Spring 1961): 95–104.

Case, Victoria, and Robert Ormond Case. *We Called It Culture: The Story of Chautauqua.* Garden City, N.Y.: Doubleday, 1948.

Cook, Charles Olson. "Boosterism and Babbitry: Charles Hillman Brough and the 'Selling' of Arkansas." *Arkansas Historical Quarterly* 37 (Spring 1978): 74–83.

———. "'The Glory of the Old South and the Greatness of the New': Reform and the Divided Mind of Charles Hillman Brough." *Arkansas Historical Quarterly* 34 (Autumn 1975): 227–41.

Cook, Larry. "Charles Hillman Brough and the Good Roads Movement in Arkansas." *Ozark Historical Review* 6 (Spring 1977): 26–35.

Cortner, Richard C. *A Mob Intent on Death: The naacp and the Arkansas Riot Cases.* Middleton, Conn., 1988.

Crawford, Charles Wann. "From Classroom to State Capitol: Charles H. Brough and the Campaign of 1916." *Arkansas Historical Quarterly* 21 (Autumn 1962): 213–30.

Dabney, Charles W. *Universal Education in the South.* 2 vols. Chapel Hill: University of North Carolina Press, 1936.

Dabney, Virginius. *Below the Potomac: A Book about the New South.* New York: Appleton-Century Co., 1942.

Dictionary of American Biography. New York: Charles Scribner's Sons, 1928–1937.

Dolmetsch, Carl R. *The Smart Set: A History and Anthology.* New York: Dial Press, 1966.

Donovan, Timothy P., and Willard Gatewood Jr., eds. *The Governors of Arkansas.* Fayetteville: University of Arkansas Press, 1981.

Duvall, Leland, ed. *Arkansas: Colony and State.* Little Rock, Ark.: Rose Publishing Co., 1973.

Encyclopedia of Southern Baptists. 2 vols. Nashville: Broadman Press, 1958.

Garner, James Wilford. *Reconstruction in Mississippi.* Baton Rouge: Louisiana State University Press, 1968. Reprint of 1901 edition.

Gould, Lewis L. *Progressives and Prohibitionists: Texas Democrats in the Wilson Era.* Austin: University of Texas Press, 1973.

Grantham, Dewey W. *The Life and Death of the Solid South: A Political History.* Lexington: University of Kentucky Press, 1988.

———. *Southern Progressivism: The Reconciliation of Progress and Tradition.* Knoxville: University of Tennessee Press, 1983.

Halliburton, R., Jr. "The Adoption of Arkansas' Anti-Evolution Law." *Arkansas Historical Quarterly* 23 (Autumn 1964): 271–83.

Harrison, Harry P., and Karl Detzer. *Culture under Canvas: The Story of Tent Chautauqua.* New York, 1958.

Hawkins, Hugh. *Pioneer: A History of the Johns Hopkins University, 1874–1889.* Ithaca, N.Y.: Cornell University Press, 1960.

Herndon, Dallas T., ed. *Centennial History of Arkansas*. 3 vols. Chicago-Little Rock: S. J. Clarke Publishing Co., 1922.

Hesseltine, William B. *Lincoln and the War Governors*. New York: Alfred A. Knopf, 1955.

Jacoway, Peggy. *First Ladies of Arkansas*. Kingsport, Tenn.: Southern Publications, Inc., 1941.

Kemler, Edgar. *The Irreverent Mr. Mencken*. Boston: Little Brown, 1950.

Key, V. O., Jr. *Southern Politics in State and Nation*. New York: Alfred A. Knopf, 1949.

Kirby, Jack Templeton. *Darkness at the Dawning: Race and Reform in the Progressive South*. Philadelphia: J. B. Lippincott Co., 1972.

Ledbetter, Calvin R., Jr. *Carpenter from Conway: George Washington Donaghey as Governor of Arkansas, 1909–1913*. Fayetteville: University of Arkansas Press, 1993.

————. "The Constitutional Convention of 1917–1918." *Arkansas Historical Quarterly* 34 (Spring 1975): 3–40.

Leflar, Robert A. *The First 100 Years: Centennial History of the University of Arkansas*. Fayetteville: University of Arkansas Foundation, Inc., 1972.

Link, Arthur S. "The Progressive Movement in the South, 1870–1917." *North Carolina Historical Review* 22 (April 1946): 172–95.

Lisenby, Foy. "The Arkansas Conference on Charities and Correction, 1912–1937." *Arkansas Historical Quarterly* 29 (Spring 1970): 39–47.

————. "Brough, Baptists, and Bombast: The Election of 1928." *Arkansas Historical Quarterly* 32 (Summer 1973): 120–31.

————. "A Survey of Arkansas's Image Problem." *Arkansas Historical Quarterly* 30 (Spring 1971): 60–71.

————. "Talking Arkansas Up: The Wonder State in the Twentieth Century." *Mid-South Folklore* 3 (Winter 1978): 85–91.

Malone, David. *Hattie and Huey: An Arkansas Tour*. Fayetteville: University of Arkansas Press, 1989.

Manchester, William. *H. L. Mencken: Disturber of the Peace*. New York: Collier Books, 1962.

McCarty, Joel. "The Red Scare in Arkansas: A Southern State and National Hysteria." *Arkansas Historical Quarterly* 37 (Autumn 1978): 264–77.

McMath, Anne. *First Ladies of Arkansas*. Little Rock, Ark.: August House, 1989.

Murray, Gail S. "Forty Years Ago: The Great Depression Comes to Arkansas." *Arkansas Historical Quarterly* 29 (Winter 1970): 291–312.

Niswonger, Richard L. *Arkansas Democratic Politics, 1896–1920*. Fayetteville: University of Arkansas Press, 1990.

Reynolds, John Hugh, and David Yancey Thomas. *History of the University of Arkansas*. Fayetteville, Ark., 1910.

Roberts, Richard, and Richard Sadler. *Ogden: Junction City*. Woodland Hills, Calif.: Windsor Publications, Inc., 1985.

Rogers, J. S. *History of Arkansas Baptists.* Little Rock: Baptist State Convention, 1948.

Rogers, O. A., Jr. "The Elaine Race Riots of 1919." *Arkansas Historical Quarterly* 29 (Summer 1960): 142–50.

Ross, Frances Mitchell. "The New Woman as Club Woman and Social Activist in Turn of the Century Arkansas." *Arkansas Historical Quarterly* 50 (Winter 1991): 317–51.

Schwitalla, Alexis Wade, comp. *Who's Who in Little Rock, 1921.* Little Rock, Ark.: New Era Press, 1921.

Senn, Gerald. "Molders of Thought, Directors of Action: The Arkansas Council of Defense, 1917–1919." *Arkansas Historical Quarterly* 36 (Autumn 1977): 280–90.

Skates, John Ray. *Mississippi: A Bicentennial History.* New York, 1979.

Sobel, Robert, ed. *Biographical Directory of the Governors of the United States, 1789–1978.* 4 vols. Westport, Conn., 1978.

Stinnett, T. M., and Clara B. Kennan. *All This and Tomorrow Too.* Little Rock: Arkansas Education Association, 1969.

Taylor, Elizabeth. "The Woman Suffrage Movement in Arkansas." *Arkansas Historical Quarterly* 15 (Spring 1956): 17–52.

Thomas, David Yancey, ed. *Arkansas and Its People: A History, 1541–1930.* 4 vols. New York: American Historical Society, 1930.

Tindall, George Brown. *The Emergence of the New South, 1913–1945.* Baton Rouge: Louisiana State University Press, 1967.

Towns, Stuart. "A Louisiana Medicine Show: The Kingfish Elects an Arkansas Senator." *Arkansas Historical Quarterly* 25 (Summer 1966): 117–27.

Waskow, Arthur I. *From Race Riot to Sit-In, 1919 and the 1960s: A Study in the Connections between Conflict and Violence.* Garden City, N.Y.: Doubleday & Co., 1967.

Wegener, Janice, ed., *Historical Report of the Secretary of State, Arkansas, 1978.* 4 vols. Little Rock, Ark., 1978.

Widener, Ralph W., Jr. "Charles Hillman Brough." *Arkansas Historical Quarterly* 34 (Summer 1975): 99–121.

Williams, Fay. *Arkansans of the Years.* 4 vols. Little Rock: C. C. Allard and Associates, 1951.

Williams, T. Harry. *Huey Long.* New York: Alfred A. Knopf, 1969.

Woodward, C. Vann. *Origins of the New South, 1877–1913.* Baton Rouge: Louisiana State University Press, 1951.

Younger, Edward, ed. *The Governors of Virginia, 1860–1978.* Charlottesville, Va., 1982.

Newspapers

Arkansas Democrat.
Arkansas Gazette.
Clipping File, General Manuscript File, History Commission, Little Rock.
Conway (Arkansas) *Log Cabin Democrat.*
Fayetteville (Arkansas) *Daily Democrat.*
Fort Smith Times-Record.
Ogden (Utah) *Standard.*

Unpublished Sources

Arsenault, Raymond Ostby. "From Populism to Progressivism in Selected Southern States: A Statistical Reinterpretation." Senior thesis, Princeton University, 1969.

Bierwirth, Elizabeth Bentley. "A Rhetorical and Semantic Study of Charles Hillman Brough's Major Chautauqua Address." M.A. thesis, University of Arkansas, 1959.

Cook, Charles Orson. "Arkansas's Charles Hillman Brough, 1876–1935: An Interpretation." Ph.D. diss., University of Houston, 1980.

Crawford, Charles Wann. "Charles H. Brough: Educator and Politician." M.A. thesis, University of Arkansas, 1957.

Ferguson, Bessie. "The Elaine Race Riot." M.A. thesis, George Peabody College, 1927.

Moyers, David Michael. "Arkansas Progressivism: The Legislative Record." Ph.D. diss., University of Arkansas, 1986.

Neal, Nevin Emil. "A Biography of Joseph T. Robinson." Ph.D. diss., University of Oklahoma, 1958.

Index